TRIBE

MADE IN BRITAIN

A Personal History of British Subculture

Martin Roach, Ian Snowball & Pete McKenna

Published by Music Press Books
an imprint of John Blake Publishing Ltd,
3 Bramber Court, 2 Bramber Road,
London W14 9PB, England

www.johnblakebooks.com
www.facebook.com/johnblakebooks
twitter.com/jblakebooks

This edition published in 2015

ISBN: 978 1 90619 129 0

British Library Cataloguing-in-Publication Data:
A catalogue record for this book is available from the British Library.

Design by www.freshlemon.com.au
Printed in Great Britain by TJ International Ltd

1 3 5 7 9 10 8 6 4 2

Papers used by John Blake Publishing are natural, recyclable
products made from wood grown in sustainable forests.
The manufacturing processes conform to the environmental
regulations of the country of origin.

Every attempt has been made to contact the relevant copyright-holders,
but some were unobtainable. We would be grateful if the appropriate
people could contact us.

Contents

Kindly supported by

#STANDFORSOMETHING

INTRODUCTION

By Martin Roach

Some time back in 2011, I received an email from a certain Ian Snowball, aka Snowy. He told me that along with his writing partner, Pete McKenna, he was working on a book about British youth culture, specifically the so-called 'Tribes' such as Mods, skinheads, Northern Soul etc. He was enquiring if I would like to publish it on my own label, Independent Music Press. Completely coincidentally, I was also working on a similar title, covering the tribal landscape of subculture through first-hand interviews with people who had actually been involved at the grass-roots level. We chatted over email about our seemingly competing books and then, wishing each other well, went off to work separately on our respective projects.

A while later, a parcel arrived in the post; it was a copy of Snowy and Pete's book, *Once Upon A Tribe*, which they had completed and had published. Just as discussed, it contained scores of excellent interviews, all told first-hand, from a selection of people who had been part of these tribes. On the surface, I should've been gutted, because my own book on the same subject was not yet complete. However, instead I was fascinated. Why? Because although our two books were in theory almost identical, reading through their brilliantly energised volume, I realised just how subjective and personal this whole topic is.

Of course, there are certain accepted and defined histories of tribes, where skinheads came from, what early Mods were trying to achieve, approximate dates, iconic albums from the genre, generally acknowledged clothing styles and so on. However, as I continued to read their book and also compile my own, it was also apparent that each story was pretty much unique to each individual. This certainly applied to each account we had separately collected, but I realised that it also described my own, as well as Snowy and Pete's, at times very conflicting experiences of subculture.

So, most obviously for example, Snowy and Pete had many entries about Mods and Northern Soul. For me, being brought up in the West Midlands in the '70s and '80s (and just too young for the first wave of punk), Northern Soul made no impact whatsoever on me. I didn't know a single person in my circles who was into that scene. That's not to say there weren't any in my town, but just that I didn't know them. There were Mods, of course, but not many and in fact Scooter Boys were more predominant than an archetypal Mod. However, by contrast, my childhood *was* populated by Goths, lots of them, as well as punks and grebos – the latter being a tribe which came to have a huge impact on my adult life.

Yet when I spoke to Snowy and Pete about Goths and Grebos, they were equally as unmoved as I had been about Northern Soul. 'Goth? Nah, that's not really something I came across that much,' said Snowy. 'Surely you were around Casuals, Mart?' asked Pete.

I wasn't. I know now that Casuals were very prevalent in the Midlands in the '80s, but again not in my circles. This fact almost perplexed my two co-editors because that particular football-focussed tribe had played a very prominent part in their lives, Interestingly, Glam was a tribe that all of us had very little experience of, 'Oh, all that make-up, brrrr....' said Snowy. I only knew one kid who was into glam, hence the solitary entry in this book. None of us had real first-hand experience of Teds, although this was mostly due to our respective ages.

So, we came up with the idea of a new book, one that combined our own individual tribal experiences. We would include my Goths and grebos, alongside their Mods and Soulies. If we didn't have any experience of influences from a certain tribe, we wouldn't include it. This was *our personal account*.

That is why this book is called 'A Personal History of British Youth Culture'. If you want an all-encompassing, academically inspired and beautifully observed history of *all* the tribes, then this book is not for you (if that is the case, I would humbly recommend that you read Ted Polhemus's definitive account, *Street Style*, which is in my opinion, without equal).

Just as the choice of tribes varied between us, then so too do our opinions about those tribes and also the current state of, and future for, these subcultures. Snowy and Pete's Introduction that follows explains very clearly that they have real concerns about the lack of tribes, about the dearth of quality new music, and about a sterilisation of the live scene and so on. I don't agree with them, in many ways. I agree that the tribes do not exist in such neatly compartmentalised forms as they used to, but I do believe they have been mutated, changed by the social media age and now infinitely more complex and less easy to define. I also think there are countless examples of amazing new music and brilliant live shows. This is the point of this book, it is a written discussion, an account of a very subjective topic and ultimately, as Snowy and Pete put it, one that is all down to individual experiences.

There are many tribes that are missing from this book – Teds being an obvious one. That was, of course, the tribe that kick-started youth subculture in many respects. It would be fantastic if this book inspired someone out there to write their own collection of stories from the tribes that mattered to them and their friends that are not covered in this book, thus creating an on-going organic record.

I agree with my two collaborators that there will most likely be not many, if any 'new' tribes in the old school sense of the word. Where previously a person was defined by their choice of albums that week, their distinctive clothes, someone from a certain tribe or with a certain look that you'd cross the road to avoid. However, in my opinion, this is because the goalposts have changed – social media has meant that whereas in years gone by it might take you months or even years to find out about a tribe or band, now it can all be done in an instant. The exchange of ideas between people about music, clothing, fashion and so on is the same, it is just that now it is instantaneous, the speed of exchange of ideas is exponentially faster.

Also, by definition youth subcultures and tribes exist partly fuelled by the notion of destroying what came before, so any new tribe will always pride itself on being different to the preceding one (not exclusively, of course). I remember going to an old metalhead's house and standing as he proudly showed me two bedrooms full of vinyl records, taking up acres of shelved wall space. I went home and looked at my sizeable CD collection, which took up a fraction of the space, and it felt like an important yet symbolic difference. Fast-forward a decade or so, and an iPod with thousands of songs can fit in your pocket (I must admit, I am completely won over by the digital age and the culture of downloading, but I know this is a contentious issue, again something very personal).

What I could never disagree with Snowy and Pete about was the absolute passion that the contributors to this book wrote with. Each article may disagree about exact dates and shirt styles etc, but they all have one thing very much in common – an overwhelming and fiercely proud passion for their subject.

With this acute sense of passion and personality in mind, we decided not to edit each article into a grammatically correct, technical exercise in the English language. This, we felt, would strip much of the character and individuality out of the words. So you may very well find inconsistencies between spellings, tenses, and certainly a few words that might not officially be in the English Dictionary (!), but please read these idiosyncracies in the spirit in which they were retained – to keep that fantastic passion alive. (On that note, I must say I have been blown away by Snowy and Pete's passion for the topic as a whole and also their seemingly never-ending work-rate and diligence. I think that they are two of the most passionate and knowledgeable writers on the subject of youth culture that I have come across and I thank them for their collaboration.)

So, please, enjoy reading these articles and hearing first-hand what these people – all actual members of these tribes – write about, talk about, remember and love. You will find yourself agreeing with many ideas and stories, and no doubt, disagreeing with some, too. That paradox just reinforces the focus of this title – to offer a voice for these highly subjective and colourful experiences of subcultural life. It is all about the individual.

Martin Roach, November 2015.

INTRODUCTION

by Ian Snowball and Pete McKenna

Living in the United Kingdom, eh! What other nation can boast such a rich and impressive youth culture? We have a youth culture linked together by music, passion and fashion. Nowhere else can boast the same! This book is a celebration and dedication to some of the most diverse, passionate and individual street culture tribes to have sprung up in the UK since the '60s. A frank, colourful recollection written by those who were there – and many who still are – from a variety of people who know what it's like to be a part of the scene and continue to live their lives by it. Visually the difference between these tribes could not be more apparent, but deep down, where it matters, they all share a common, generic DNA. Obsessive attention to detail when it comes down to clothes and style, a passion for their particular music and an attitude that sticks an irreverent two fingers up to world in general, plus a special, close camaraderie for everyone in their scene.

In our opinion, this book only exists because of two major cultural shifts in British social history that helped to change the attitudes and landscape of this once green and pleasant land

11

forever, for better, for worse. I'm talking about the abolition of conscription and the 'turn on, tune in, drop out', sex, drugs, rock and roll bloodless revolution that was the '60s. Ever since Boadicea fought the Roman invaders, the UK has been a warrior island race and up until fairly recent times has fought a war every thirty years or so in the name of King, Queen and country.

Battlefields the world over are strewn with the corpses of young English youth who were offered no choice but to sign up, rally to the flag and march off to foreign lands to do their bit. The abolition of conscription changed all that overnight. It offered the new generation an option previously denied to generations past. Those wanting to join up and fight could willingly pack up their troubles in their old kit bag, kiss goodbye to family, friends and loved ones and march off to glory. Those who didn't could remain at home without being labelled unpatriotic cowards, afraid to show their faces down the local, just in case one of their school chums was reported to have paid the ultimate price.

The Second World War had cost Britain dearly, almost bringing her down to the knees of bankruptcy. Years of hardship and poverty were the way of life long after the last bullet had been fired in anger, continuing into the '50s as the country finally managed to claw itself back to its feet in order to offer the new generation a glimmer of hope, of better financially secure times ahead. The arrival of the '60s heralded an unprecedented wave of social change, much to the disgust of the old school, dyed-in-the-wool establishment who'd controlled the country and the lives of the people in it for centuries. Unlike America, who continued to recruit and send its young men off to fight and die in the swamps and snake-infested jungles of Vietnam, British kids were having a ball of a time enjoying a sense of freedom, attitude and individuality that their predecessors were denied.

They had education, secure jobs, apprenticeships, cash in their pockets, dreams and ambitions and mobility as they stuck a firm two fingers up to the old order while searching for their own identities and values and a fair number of kicks to match. Admittedly the '50s spawned the Teddy Boys, Rockers and Beatniks, each of them with their own distinctive music and look, much of it heavily influenced (if not in total) by the good old USA. Live and let live, each to their own and all that but for us, the emergence of the Mod scene epitomised the definition of cool youthful attitude and style that set the benchmark for future tribes to follow.

Thank God the Mods looked to European/Italian/French influences instead of following the time-honoured prescription of the Stars and Stripes to show them the way forward. Sharp, expensive tailor-made suits in the finest materials with footwear and haircuts to match. Instead of souped-up gas guzzlers and ape hanger choppers, they opted for Italian scooters, Vespas, Lambrettas, adopting a way of thinking that it's not how fast you get there, it's how you arrive and that was *everything*. Nights spent down sweaty clubs dropping speed and dancing to the home-grown and imported R 'n' B soul music that set another fresh new benchmark for a different generation to follow. Then came Brighton, May Bank Holiday 1964, and the mass battles on the beaches between the Mods, Rockers and police. Then the original Mod scene had died a death, many of them moving on to the new acid/dope/free sex and love scene sweeping all corners of the UK but we must never ever forget the attitudes and style of those pre-64 Mods who continue to live on today and hopefully forever more.

Linked in so many ways to the early Mod scene, the next big street cred tribe to hit the streets were the Skinheads. Hard Mods, as some of the early skins preferred to be called, stuck true to the old Mod ethics but doing it in a different way. Bethnal Green 1966 was the place where the first mob of skins were seen on the streets. Grandad shirts, Ben Shermans, Fred Perrys, braces, hobnail boots and Levi's. How fearsome to the general public must they have looked, swaggering, barging their way through everyone and everything without a care in the world, on their way to the dancehall for a piss up on the Ska and reggae, long before the skinhead army grew in numbers across the nation, every city, town and village boasting its own skin army.

The skins were effectively Mods without scooters, sharing so many similarities to their predecessors. A love of black music, booze and speed to help them dance the night away. Sharp clothes and attention to detail and seaside weekends battling with the bikers and other rival skinhead gangs. Setting the seeds that grew into the mass hooligan football riots that were a big part of '70s youth culture and, also, the more streamlined undercover football hooligan battles of the '80s, courtesy of the good old mobile phone. Of course, the '70s skins received bad press when some of them turned to far right-wing politics. On a plus note, skins were responsible for championing a little known Northampton footwear manufacture, the firm's name Dr. Martens, who produced the iconic eight and ten hole black and cherry red stitch-up AirWair sole bovver boot, now worn by rich and famous celebrities the world over.

There was nothing more scary than seeing a bunch of skins marching down the road for a night out and from that classic shaven-headed, denim wearing, Doc Martens bovver boot image, the skins spawned several new tribes similar in attitude and fashion who did things a little different. The boneheads who went one step further in their quest to be different. The Suedeheads, skinheads with longer hair, were imbued with the same swagger and meticulous attention to detail when it came down to fashion. Even the designer hungry Casuals and hoolies of the '80s who proved themselves to be a constant and embarrassing thorn in Maggie Thatcher's side every time England played away, owed their existence to the early skins. Same attitude with a different uniform, as expensive prized designer names came to the forefront of the new culture: Fila, Lacoste, Sergio Tacchini, Nike, Adidas, Kappa, Burberry, Aquascutum, John Smedley, Ralph Lauren and Stone Island.

What more can be written that hasn't already been written about the Northern Soul scene? This is the longest existing underground dance scene this country has spawned, stretching back to the early '60s when sharp-suited Mods danced the night away to the new, imported soul sounds in West End clubs such as The Flamingo and The Scene. Unlike most scenes that started out with a word and a whisper where to go, the Northern Soul scene has shunned the limelight and still remains a scene where you have to know where to look for it. The music gradually drifted to the north of England, finding a welcome home in cities and towns steeped in the faded heritage of the Industrial Revolution. The Golden Torch in Tunstall Stoke, the Catacombs in Birmingham, Samantha's in Sheffield, the VaVa's in Bolton, the Highland Room in Blackpool and, inevitably so, the legendary Casino Soul Club in Wigan where it remained the headquarters of the scene from 1973 to December 1981 when a fire destroyed the heart and soul of the Northern Soul world.

It was largely a working-class dance scene populated by guys and girls who took themselves and the music they loved very seriously indeed, creating an image and attitude all of their own. There was a stereotypical image of a Northern Soulie – long leather coat, baggy trousers, berets, tee shirts and the girls' long, flared skirts, low cut tight tops and white socks – but fashion didn't mean a thing on the Northern Soul scene, but being there did. Poor guys and girls mixed with those more fortunate, wearing what they could just be a part of the scene and everyone came together under the ghostly glow of the ultra violet strip light to dance the night away soaked in amphetamine soul sweat. Words can only come close to describing what the feeling was like when the Casino was running on all engines, packed to the rafters and everyone on the dance-floor dancing like demons from dusk till dawn. End of!

Mods are a British phenomenon, so are skinheads, Suedeheads,

Teddy boys, the Northern Soulies, Ravers of the second Summer of Love (Hippies of the first) and the football Casuals, to mention just a few. They are the lost tribes of a mis-spent youth. Did they crop up in France, Germany, America?... there's no evidence to say so, is there? So being a young person in Britain throughout the '50s up until the early or mid-90s meant you would be exposed to 'the tribes'. This did not mean you had to be British either though, or working class, middle class or white. You just needed to be exposed to it. So we do not hold an opinion that someone has to be British to be a Mod, Skin, Casual etc, but we do not believe these things could have been born anywhere else other than in the United Kingdom. But, like we say, this is only our opinion.

Mark Smith once said, 'Some of us chose to pick the pocket of the past'. That's what the bands of the 78/79 Mod era done. That's what many of us still do today and frequently seek out vintage clobber or records on eBay and the charity shops. For many a young person in the late '70s and early '80s the bands like the Purple Hearts, Secret Affair and, of course, The Jam were the gateway back towards the '60s bands of The Small Faces, The Creation and The Action. Not very forward looking, eh... or Modernist thinking for that matter but it worked because of the attitude, passion and angst of the British youth of those grey days. 'Pick those pockets' we did eagerly and still do.

Several contributions in this book refer to the importance of *Top of the Pops*, *The Tube*, *Ready Steady Go*, the Top 40 charts on Sundays. Teenagers lived their lives and made their choices according to what they heard, what they liked, what they could buy. What do the kids have today?

Now don't get us wrong, we also take advantage of YouTube and Facebook and Myspace or use the brilliant online sites like Soul Source but our foundations are firmly in place. They should be after years of listening, discovering and contributing to the 'scenes'. In our opinion the youth of today is missing out on something so special because they do not have *Top of the Pops*,

The Tube and the like. 'Dance, dance, dance to the radio' sang Ian Curtis, and for decades the kids did.

In our opinion, there has not been much quality bursting out of the music biz in recent years. Of course, there are exceptions like the Artic Monkeys or The Libertines to name just two from recent years… but we could probably only add a handful more to the list. But our question is, will there ever be any iconic albums again? *Searching For The Young Soul Rebels* comes to mind. I just cannot see it, 'Where have you hidden them?'

Plus, in my opinion, going to a gig does not offer the raw power and energy that it used to. What with a million security guards and health and safety rules it's hard to fart without someone taking offence. We have never complained when some drunken nutter has spilt beer down our backs or dropped a hot rock onto our shirt. Snowy never complained when one of the members of a band jumped into the audience at a gig in Bristol that he drove to with a bunch of mates on a Wednesday evening (we lived in Kent so it was not just around the corner) and broke his nose as he landed on him. Snowy still has the scar and bent nose to prove it. For us, these were the type of experiences that raw gigs had to offer and made us hungry for more.

It appears to us that it has all gone a bit too TAME. The live music of any decade or generation reflects its youth groups. When we hear The Jam, The Clash or Joy Division… and this list can go on much further as we are transported back to the feel of the times and the type of youths that lived in them days. We are not saying it was all perfect and we do not intend for this to appear like we are looking through rose-tinted glasses and dribbling nostalgia, we all know the real truth.

And it goes on. Where have the record shops gone? The traditional corner pubs and the menswear shops? These examples were places that young people went to so they could keep up to speed with what was 'in'. They were meeting places to check one another out. We all know the sound and feel of a

33rpm is better, warmer than any CD or any other such format. Putting a record on the deck was like a ritual. It was a process. A journey! What happens now has less charm. Just press the button or push the disc in the hole! No crackles, no anticipation, no effort.

Effort was a large part of being a Mod or Casual or so on. To be a member of a tribe meant you had to devote time, money and energy to getting the 'look' right. But we enjoyed doing it. We had pride. We looked forward to the weekend gig, disco or match to sport our new shirt, coat or trainers.

So what else helped kill off the tribes? Was it something in the water? Not exactly, but it was as if something was in the air. Rave. The second Summer of Love – 1988 or 1989 (depends who you talk to). Many of us were a part of it and therefore contributed to it. It all happened very fast. There were pockets of the old tribes in corners of discos and cafes and then the raves arrived. Within months it appeared that the whole nation was scooped up by its energy and momentum and then a year later it had run out of steam, in the same way that people say Punk only really lasted six months. This left a generation waiting for the next thing... we do not believe there has been a 'next thing' yet, and suspect that these times, society and young people have changed so much that there will never be another 'next thing'... a TRIBE.

Will there ever be a return to youth culture's stylish tribes? We think doubtful, certainly not on the mass scale that the previous four decades have witnessed. We cannot see how all the time that youth has no real passion for music and the clothes they wear that will set them apart from the boring masses. Our society today has too many ideas that care not for style. It's no-one's fault, it's just not as important as it was to the British youth of the '50s, '60s, '70s and '80s.

Each contribution is also a personal celebration of the individual's youth. It is also an admission to their passion for the music, fashion and the era that they grew up with and participated in. Who knows, perhaps a thousand years from now historians will read this book, and our preceding sister title, *Once Upon A Tribe*, and understand the truth about Mods, Casuals, Soulies and so on. In the compiling of the book I learnt a lot from the people I spoke with. The labels attached are more often than not attached by those (like the media) looking from the outside inwards. It's common knowledge now that many Mods in the '60s did not refer to themselves as Mods at all. So perception is everything and the tribes were not built on labels but on passion, attitude and wanting something different than just a nine-to-five, a week's holiday in Spain every year and a new fireplace for their two-up-two-down. The tribes belong to something different. It's hard to communicate in words alone but those involved will know what is being referred to because of a special feeling.

The tribes wanted to be noticed. Most of us will know that feeling that we get when we enter a club in a new shirt or new pair of trainers. We want others to notice us. Casuals know it, Mods know it, all of the tribes know it. Perhaps it stemmed from the working classes wanting to get noticed and because they could not do it with a flash motor, they chose to do it with style and attitude instead.

This book is in no way meant to be a comprehensive account of every British youth subculture that ever roamed Albion. It is only a crude account of the lives of thousands of young people. Young people that use to hang around in cafes, discos, youth clubs and street corners.

So for those who were not paying attention as a teenager or lived on the Isle of Nowhere Important, what is a Mod, skin, Casual or some of the other youth tribes? So much has been written before on the subject and really the contributions in this book explain what these tribes are in great, accurate detail. But in a brief and crude way we can add a few things to help put things into some kind of context and we will only mention some of the tribes to give a flavour and set the tone. When you read the actual contributions in the book, you will be hopefully be left with a more informed understanding of what they were/are.

And so as the memories and interviews arrived from the contributors that we were talking too, a common thread and feel revealed itself. It was obvious that everybody was writing about the same thing. It was their personal relationship and love of music, clothes and the part that these had in their own personal youth. The book was taking on a presence full of richness because the honest words being written came from deep down in the hearts of the contributors. What happened was that the book turned into the participants of youth culture writing about youth culture from within looking out and not from the outside looking in. We didn't write the interviews and text in this book, we only compiled the contributions.

This is why it is so important to stress that this book is a *personal* account and not a definitive, objective record. I [Snowy] remember when I quizzed Pete McKenna over the use of talcum powder at the Wigan Casino. He said in all the years from 74 to 81 that he attended the Casino, not once did he see any talc on the floor. This is Pete's experience where as someone else may say they did see talc at the club. Both are right because both had their experience. Even when inviting people to contribute to the book, a couple of people wanted to but backed out. When they were asked why they said they didn't want to put their 'heads on the block' and have others judge them by saying things like, 'Who do they think they are?' The response they got from the three editors was, 'Just write about what you know, what you did, because those experiences are unique to you and nobody can take that away from you.'

Ian Snowball and Pete McKenna, November 2015.

BIKERS

*Ken, a very honest and emotional
account of an early Biker's experiences.*

I got my first bike in the March of 1977. It wasn't new, far from
it, but that didn't matter, as it was British. It had to be British and,
for me, it had to have non-standard, raised handle bars. We had all
seen Chopper style bikes. Although fairly scarce, Choppers had
been around for years, and we had all seen the film *Easy Rider* that
had come out about six years earlier. We could not afford to go
the full custom route to turn our bikes into Choppers, but that
was – and is – the style of bike we liked. For us then, big bars were
where to start, and a step in the right direction.

My mates had already got their bikes months earlier as they'd
turned 17 (the watershed age limit) before me. Now, here we
were, seven of us, all with our 250cc machines (as you could
ride on 'L' plates in them days), and all ready to create madness
and mayhem (or so we thought ha ha ha). We all loved AC/DC,
Deep Purple, Saxon, Hawkwind and my particular favourite,
Motörhead. We hated disco and Punk with a passion. We called

ourselves 'The Malevolent Seven', and had painted the same with white poster paints on the backs of our cut-offs in an inverted horse shoe shape. We thought we were the beez knees.

My bike was a 1965 BSA C10 250, as were the bikes of two others in our group. All three beezas were gloss black with chrome spoked wheels and chrome panels on the tanks. Another mate, Tommo, had a Triumph Trailblazer 250 in mustard yellow, and another, Mickey, had a pale metalic blue Triumph Tiger Cub 200cc.

We thought these British bikes were proper bike porn, although we all dreamt of passing our tests and graduating up to a Triumph Bonneville 650. The other two in our group, Wills and JJ, both rode Honda CB250s, but also dreamt of one day owning a big Brit twin. We tried not to hold the owning of Jap bikes against Wills and JJ too much (at least their bikes were four stroke, not screeching two strokes, like the Yamaha RD250s and Suzuki GT250s that the trendy kids screamed about on), but we did rib them quite a lot about their bikes.

We called ourselves either Greasers or Bikers, depending on the mood (Bikers as a name was just coming in and was a name we liked, as to be a Biker you had to have a bike, but a Greaser could be a Greaser without a bike). We never called ourselves Rockers. We styled ourselves on the Hells Angels that we had once seen riding in an awe-inspiring pack along the Kings Road in Chelsea. They were our GODS.

Our hair was long, and looking back, very lank, and we wore deliberately filthy flared Levi's jeans, Brando-style leather jackets (except Mickey who wore an old sheep-skin lined ex-RAF pilots jacket that he got from his uncle), but unlike the Rockers we saw as kids in the '60s, we wore our bike badges and regalia on sleeveless Levi's jackets (had to be Levi's) that we wore over the tops of our leathers, rather than fastened to them. I liked this look a lot.

On hot days we would wear these sleeveless cut-offs over our tee shirts. This made Mickey look like his mum had dressed him, as his cut-off was much bigger than ours by necessity, as it had to fit over his huge sheepskin lined jacket. We always ribbed Mickey over this, but if anyone else did, we would to a man (well, to a seventeen-year-old teenager) stand up for him.

We used to drive like dervishes to and from a range of places like the last few transport cafes that were open on the A406 and A13, the Wimpey Bar in Romford, and the Rock Nights that took place out in the sticks at a range of youth clubs in and around Essex and Hertfordshire. It was while we were riding to one of these gigs that Mickey crashed into a tractor and trailer, on a bend, in the half-light of dusk, as we rode through Essex. I still miss Mickey to this day...

Ken.

★ ★ ★

Anon – a neat summary of biker culture, literature and events.

My mates and I have been what some would call 'Life-Style' Bikers since 1985 when we first saw a copy of the (then) newly launched British bike magazine, *Back Street Heroes*. My contemporaries and I had been riding non-standard bikes of one sort or another since the start of that decade, and found our passion for MAD modified motorcycles – which encompassed all shapes, makes, and sizes – more than admirably catered for by this magazine.

For *Back Street Heroes* magazine was a tonic to our soul. It was totally street, totally cred, and represented 100% the biker scene that was happening at root level in Britain, and operated against the socially stagnant, strike-filled political back-drop of Tory-led mid-80s Britain. Unlike some of the advertising-lead glossy motorcycle mags which had ruled the roost prior to the arrival of *Back Street Heroes* (notwithstanding *Motorcycle Mechanics* magazine, which was ace), *Back Street Heroes* was written by low-budget genuine Bikers, for ordinary street cred low-budget Bikers. The magazine fuelled the fire to spread the word, and as the word spread, so did the popularity and circulation of the mag, to such an extent, that by the later '80s, the question arose, which came first, the chicken or the egg?

You see in those pre-internet, pre-Facebook, and pre-Twitter (whatever that is) days, *Back Street Heroes* magazine became a social glue shared by all in the British Biker world (and beyond), and even if you weren't in regular 'real time' contact with like-minded Bikers, through the pages of *Back Street Heroes*, you felt yourself to be a part of a totally supportive, sub-cultural Brother (or Sister)-hood...

One testimony to the importance of *BSH* for the '80s Biker scene is/was the fantastic success, and year-on-year growth that decade saw, of the large-scale Biker events, organised by real Bikers, for Bikers, rather than the seemingly false and slick large-scale events that had been attempted by an array of A&R men prior to the arrival of *BSH* here in the U.K.

Perfect examples of such events include the now legendary Kent Custom Bike Show weekend (now sadly no longer on the calendar), the Bath & West Custom Bike Show weekend (similarly, sadly now no longer on the Biker calendar), and the Bull Dog Bash, which takes place just outside of Stratford-upon-Avon in August, which as an event, notwithstanding 2013 when it had a year off, is still on-going and as popular ever. All the events as detailed were (and in the case of the Bull Dog Bash, are) organised and run by members of the Hells Angels Motorcycle Club and their associates.

These rallies/custom show weekends would attract thousands and thousands of Biker revellers, would include open air festival-style live music gigs from prominent bands and musicians, which in turn would see said events getting lots of column inches in

BSH, which in turn would generate a greater gate presence for the next such event, and so on ...

The British (and European) Biker scene in the '80s was BREATHTAKINGLY brilliant, and I wouldn't've missed being involved for the world. The scene is still strong though, although these days it seems more macro, with many, many hundreds of smaller Biker weekends filling almost every weekend, the length and breadth of Europe, rather than a few well-placed large-scale events dominating the Biker calendar: I guess being an organic movement, change was – and is – inevitable?

My crew and I still hammer on down to a range of Biker camping rally and Rock weekends each year however, and even though we are now the grave-side of 50, plan on doing so for as long as we can still ride. For unlike many other movements which see its members come and go, being a Life-Style Biker is an on-going and inspirational Way of Life that has become an intrinsic part of our daily DNA.

Anonymous.

★ ★ ★

Author Gary Charles, extracted from his acclaimed book, Bikers.

By the '70s, the international Biker movement had started to spread beyond America and Britain. In many countries such as Germany, Austria, the Benelux countries, Scandinavia, Australia and New Zealand (to name but a few), their numbers reached what the authorities perceived as being of epidemic proportions. The unified image perpetuated alongside the motorcycle at that time (which ideally had to be a chopper) was heavily influenced by *Easy Rider*, although it had been amalgamated with a cocktail of other influences including remnants of Brando's *The Wild One* and elements of Hippy fashion. Within a few years, this universal Biker image was unmistakable across the globe, with only nominal national subtleties setting each country apart. A new name started to be used by the press of the day to describe this new breed of Biker – 'The Greaser' had been officially categorised and labelled.

Hair was worn long by these Greasers, and mutton chop sideburns and later full beards grown. Jeans were unavoidably oil-stained, flared and by Levi's, and leather jackets covered with similarly oil splattered cut-offs. A cut-off or set of 'colours' (the term used to describe a given motorcycle club's particular motif and name) as they are also known, is basically a denim jacket (again preferably by Levi's) with the sleeves removed, which is worn over the top of a leather jacket to display the badges and identifying graphics of their group. Previously, these would have been fixed directly to the leather item itself. However, the separation of the cut-off from the leather jacket allowed a degree of anonymity when needed, while still maintaining the protection of the leather when riding. Then, at an appropriate time and place, the cut-off could be easily returned to its more overt location on top of the leather. By the '80s, leather cut-offs were being manufactured by tanners sympathetic to Biker life. These were more durable than their denim counterparts, and (arguably) looked a whole lot better; nonetheless examples of their denim predecessor still prevail in some quarters to this day, and probably always will.

Other aspects of the Biker culture also evolved in the '70s. Helmets – where worn and where possible – were ex-German army, and sometimes chromed and polished, but usually as standard complete with original insignias. German Iron Crosses (original and/or reproduction) were also used to adorn many cut-offs in America and Britain, as in the words of a friend of mine at that time, "Our dads fought the Germans in the War. What better way is there to piss them off than wear the medals of their enemy?" These pieces of regalia were not adopted by all Biking countries (then or now) though, for blatantly obvious reasons.

The philosophy of wearing the Iron Cross is explained further by the following transcript from an interview with a Biker called Tony, billed as a rebel rocker, from a 1969 BBC television documentary entitled *A Year In The Life*. The transcript is taken from Tony's response to being asked about his anti-social and malevolent behaviour, and brings firmly into question the mythology that the late '60s and early '70s were a time of youthful Hippy-inspired peace and tranquillity.

"What it is, is we are living in their world and we don't like it. We want to change it and the only way we can change it is by rearing up... We can't change it by talk or anything because they won't listen. They say we are not old enough or sensible enough so what you've got to do is make them feel really sick with you..."

Many Flower-Power followers were politicised at that time, with strong allegiances to the far left. Some even erred towards the West's biggest taboo: Communism. These deluded themselves that the revolution was just around the corner, and some that the international Biker fraternity was their Praetorian guard, their vanguard against suppression, and their own front line troops who would rise up and fight for them on command when the glorious day arrived. Ha ha! Obviously they had experimented a little too often with the hallucinogenic drugs that they – and others of their kidney – were purportedly trying to legalise...

Bikers were and are fiercely loyal to a cause – their cause. They would do almost anything to protect and defend it. But rise up and fight for a bunch of Hippies? Think again, mystic men, think again. True, many Bikers were political at the time, but in the main, these politics were left outside the theatre of biking, as to Bikers, the internal politics of their given calling were – and are – often more important than those outside. Coupled with the fact that most of these political agitators were viewed by Bikers as pigeon-chested wimps with whom they wanted nothing to do, if ever said activists over-stepped the mark, they ran the risk of being reminded of such via a good old-fashioned Biker-style SLAP!

Many Greasers did fight for groups in the '70s though, but not in preparation for any pending revolution. They fought against those who threatened or challenged their authority (like the Mods and Skinheads in England) or their territory, which in certain areas of the world meant fighting others of their kind.

From its earliest days, cycle culture has been dominated by gang loyalties and rivalries, as depicted in *The Wild One*. By the '90s this facet of Biker-life had escalated into a complex hierarchical club scene complete with aligned actions and etiquette. These seemingly feudal systems are far from draconian though. But before the well-evolved '90s status quo was achieved, we had the '80s, and before that, the 'Savage '70s, which can best be expressed by the following short story.

The year was 1972. For one reason or another I was in Essex, England. It was a hot sticky June evening, and I had been attracted to an event in the village of Danbury, about seven miles out from the county town of Chelmsford. Normally this was a quiet well-to-do little hamlet, but on this occasion, it was to be the staging point for a Greaser upon Greaser conflict. In what must have been the centre of the village was a large hall with a shingle car park and an adjoining field of some considerable size. Traditional '50s style Rock and Roll was blurting out from the hall as I arrived amidst the pink hue of dusk, courtesy of a most passable local band. In the car park were what seemed like hundreds of British motorbikes of all shapes, sizes and styles. These were parked in two distinctly different and demarked zones.

The hall and car park were virtually void of revellers though, as the vast majority of people appeared to be congregating in the field. A large group of spectators were gathered at the car park end, while in the middle stood what seemed like two massive groups of motorcyclists. These groups had removed their leather jackets, but replaced their cut-offs over an assortment of T-shirt and vest tops, and some seemed to be holding bike chains or spanners. On the backs of one set of cut-offs were written the words 'Billericay Bastards', and on the others 'Danbury Tigers'. This was the Tiger's patch, but the 'Billericay Bastards' believed themselves to be top dogs in Essex at that time, and were here to prove it. There then followed some shouting and gesturing before BOSH, it all went off!

The two gangs moved in on each other like so many medieval warriors. Girls in the spectator sector screamed, Bikers in the thick of it screamed, and claret ran freely as metal implement after metal implement collided purposefully with flesh and bone. After what seemed like only a couple of seconds the two groups separated, with several of their number clutching bloody heads. From where I stood there had been no clear victor, although as both teams hastily collected their gear, mounted their machines, and sped away in opposite directions ahead of the arrival of the police (whose bells were now clearly audible), each proclaimed they had spanked the other side's arse.

This had been a good old-fashioned turf war between two back patch clubs, neither of which made it past the '70s.

Gary Charles.

BRITPOP

Stuart, a first-hand witness to Britpop.

I was living in London in the late '80s and early '90s, following music, going to tons of gigs and just really enjoying being in the capital. I wasn't a mad fan of Madchester bands like the Stone Roses, I quite liked PWEI and their lot, but found grunge a little bit dull (apart from Nirvana at their best). So when the *NME* and *Melody Maker* started writing about some of the new Wave of New Wave bands and then, shortly after, British acts such as Suede and Blur, I was hooked.

Here were bands from our isle, our culture, our way of life. That was an instant appeal but it wasn't just some misguided jingoism. The music was bloody brilliant (at first anyway). Despite all the latterday recriminations and comments, *Parklife* by Blur is a bloody great album. Suede were a little too twee for me, but at the same time they need recognition for lighting the fire and Brett Andersen will always be a superb front man.

I went to scores of gigs, some increbdile, many not so brilliant, at venues like the Dublin Castle, the Underworld, The Powerhaus in Islington, all that lot. Obviously when Britpop became a 'scene' and the media latched on to it, these bands were no longer quite so accessible, and the small venues were swapped for arenas in many cases, but at first it was so vibrant and exciting.

The dress code was an odd mix. Very British in a way, Fred Perrys, Ben Shermans, Dr. Martens (oxblood or black, a few green ones, too). Harrington jackets, crombies, so there was a real sense of Mod, skinhead, Two Tone, sort of this mash-up of very cool, quite meticulous styles. I always thought Damon Albarn looked the best, personally, even though I know some people would disagree.

The surge of Britpop bands went hand in hand with a real glory days era for British music writing and magazines. There was jus so much content to be written about and the likes of *Select, NME, Melody Maker,* Q did so, for the most part, very well.

Like most scenes, once the mainstream got hold of it, the original adopters started to become disillusioned. Blur vs Oasis for the Number 1 spot was bubblegum pop news content and I can see why the BBC got involved etc. Ditto the whole Blur on *Top of the Pops* in milk floats etc. You can't blame the media or the bands. Fortunately, Blur have gone on to spread their wings way past Britpop, as have a handful of the really talented bands from that period.

Britpop is often derided in the press for being too retro, for collapsing in a haze of drugs (I'm no rock and roller but I always think that element was overplayed, there were no more drugs in that scene than in any other, if not less so to some degree – but that's a very personal issue and experience). I hope in time it will be looked at more fondly. Certainly for me, it was a golden era in my young life, when clothes, music, hair and bands really *mattered* to me and my mates.

Stuart.

★ ★ ★

Martin Roach, extracted and abridged from his book, Blur: The Whole Story.

By 1994, Britain was fully gripped by the phenomenon called Britpop, and it is worth sparing a few moments to look at this. The first thing to state and to pre-empt the discussion below is that 'Britpop' is a media fiction, a musical movement christened by outsiders and not by the bands supposedly involved. By discussing it here, I am in fact fuelling the myth. Nevertheless, labels of convenience have littered music writing since its inception and they are often necessary evils in attempting to describe and analyse this most incendiary and variable of art forms.

In 1994, there was an inspired renaissance of British music that saw a whole collection of new native bands breakthrough. Previously, against a backdrop of American slacker-driven grunge culture, British music had been largely ignored and in fact derided during the early '90s, ever since the demise of Madchester. Alongside this American rock domination, the commercial charts were swamped with one hit wonders, cover versions, novelty songs and old timers.

Many factors combined to create Britpop. Undoubtedly the arrival of Suede was a key catalyst in 1992, with their highly stylised, romantic London dramas, and Brett's peculiar camp Englishness. Pat Gilbert of *Record Collector* is a fan of Britpop and he believes Suede were essential to its inception: "Britpop's genesis has its roots in Suede, who were the first post-indie band who refused to be mulling and wantonly middle class, they didn't want to recreate three-minute perfect pop songs in the line of the Velvets and the Byrds and they came along with a bit of swagger. Suede were definitely the first time in years that English bands had reclaimed some sense of occasion about what they were doing, and people started looking back at British bands rather than all that American stuff. Suede started all that."

Nevertheless, *Modern Life Is Rubbish* was Blur's first quint-essentially English album and many of their British ideas pre-date Suede, including crucially the 'our culture is under siege' theory. What Suede had was the commercial exposure and success that gave their ideas recognition. In April of 1993, *Select* magazine ran a feature not so subtly titled "Yanks Go Home" which featured a whole list of English style bands. With Suede on the cover, there were also features on Pulp, St Etienne, Denim and The Auteurs. Notably, Blur didn't even get a mention, even though advance copies of the first of their English trilogy albums were already in circulation in the industry. The humourous piece with a prophetic undertone ran thus: "Who do you think you are kidding Mr. Cobain? Enough is enough! We don't want plaid. We want crimplene, glamour, wit and irony. If 1992 was the American year then it's time to bring on the home guard." Maybe grunge encapsulated a cultural low, that coincided with the economic depression, and perhaps with the recession fading there was a new positivity springing up which brought the resurgence of more optimistic British bands.

The home guard grew during 1993 with *Modern Life* being complemented by Suede's eponymously titled, No.1 award winning debut album. The rejuvenation of the festivals that had been helped by memorable performances by the likes of Nirvana and Pearl Jam was now taken over with stunning live shows by Blur and Suede of course, but also by The Boo Radleys and veteran British pioneers New Order. Nirvana's *Nevermind* follow up *In Utero* silenced some of the doubters for a while, but with designer grunge now prancing along the catwalks and grunge-by-numbers advertising American jeans, the voices of dissent grew.

1994 was when it all exploded. Britpop was jump-started by the energetic emergence of New Wave of New Wave at the tail end of 1993. However, once Blur's *Parklife* had pushed the NWONW aside, the flood gates of Britpop opened, and the untimely death of Kurt Cobain acted as a tragic heralding of the end of an era. Throughout 1994, streams of new bands came through, and with the mainstream media picking up on Britpop, the resurgence of British music was quite astounding. In the next splendid eighteen months, Pulp finally broke their 14 year duck and produced a sexually subversive, comical seedy masterpiece in their first major label album *His 'n' Hers*. Elastica broke away from their suffocating early NWONW status to release a volley of classic pop singles, stating the case for female writers, as did Sleeper. The Auteurs more sombre style had somewhat underachieved, but Oxford's Radiohead filled the void with an odd debut album which was soon followed by *The Bends*, universally recognised as one of the finest moments of '90s British music. At the opposite end to the saintly patience of Pulp came Supergrass, who only formed in early 1994, and within eighteen months had smashed into the album charts at No.1 with their amazing debut album *I Should Coco*. The ranks were also swelled by the likes of Shed Seven, Portishead, The Bluetones, Marion, Powder, Dodgy, and the album chart topping Boo Radleys. There was also the ultimate derivative Britpop band Menswear, who appeared on *Top of the Pops* before their first single was even released. Ironically, Suede had experienced a bad year in 1994 with the loss of guitarist and key songwriter Bernard Butler – fortunately, with the arrival of Richard Oakes as a replacement and the excellent and under-rated second album *Dog Man Star*, Suede returned from the brink. Blur at Alexandra Palace, Suede's debut album, Supergrass on *Top of the Pops* and Jarvis on *Pop Quiz* were all great Britpop moments. The Mod phenomenon also underwent something of a revival, with Modfather Paul Weller enjoying renewed success. Blur's own Mod leanings on the second album were no longer dominant but many still tagged them as part of the new movement. However you looked at it, this was a great new era for British music, and now grunge bands couldn't get arrested. Except for in America, that is.

The Britpop phenomenon caused/coincided with a resurgence in various other areas of the British music industry. For example, *Top of the Pops* had a new producer, Ric Blaxill, who single-handedly rejuvenated what had become a frequently derided programme in the early '90s. Record sales rocketed in the UK by 14% on the previous year, so that total sales reached an all time high of £1.5 billion. Also, live shows suddenly became something to see again, and 14 year olds began switching off their Nintendos and forming bands once again. Certain older bands became fashionable influences again. The majority of the great British bands draw on the unique character of British life. Just as The Sex Pistols laughed at the tabloids, The Jam detailed small town precincts and The Smiths mythologised the normality of life, now Blur and the new generation were hailing the good and bad of their home country. Many of the Britpop groups had grown up in Britain without the first hand clutter of punk, so this was barely involved, although some bands drew on it for live shows. Far more substantially, many of the '60s beat groups that were cited as references for *Modern Life* and *Parklife* now enjoyed a renewed popularity.

Vocally if not lyrically, Damon's so-called Mockney accent mirrored the Cockney Rebel Steve Harley and who else but Jarvis Cocker could sing about "wood chip" in a Sheffield accent? Cynics successfully argued that many of Britpop's contingent sounded too much like their influences, a kind of 'spot the reference', slicing up history and re-selling the same package. Defenders pointed to acts who were re-inventing the past with their own dash of originality, taking a pastiche and working it with enough intelligence to create something fresh and new.

So 1994 was the year of Britpop's arrival, with Blur's *Parklife* as the album of that year beyond question. However, if you accept that Britpop as a musical umbrella exists, then you also have to acknowledge its enormous diversity. The peculiar English musical reference points of Blur and Supergrass were hardly acceptable influences for Radiohead. Pulp and Blur talked of a behind-the-net curtains Britain, but Oasis didn't, neither did Marion. Elastica sounded as much like Menswear as Nirvana did.

Also, the vital thing to remember is that none of these bands really considered themselves to be part of a movement. There were some groups who enjoyed success on the coat-tails of the bigger bands, but that is the case for any musical movement. Suede distanced themselves from Britpop hastily, as did Marion. Oasis refused to appear on the BBC2 documentary entitled *Britpop Now* although Damon presented it and Pulp, Elastica and Menswear appeared. Britpop remains a banner of convenience to label a rich new seam of British talent. Britpop was in many ways a media fiction and, crucially, an industry compatible one.

Martin Roach.

★ ★ ★

A '90s Brit popper *and what happened next by Rob Parker.*

It's 1994 and I'm a fresh-faced 15 year old dressed in my finest Brit-pop garb: a uniform of needle cords and Adidas Sambas. I've blown my meagre paperboy's wages on a ticket to see The Charlatans at the Brixton Academy, my first real gig. Already overawed by the scale of the venue and the electric atmosphere, the band take to the stage and set my pulse racing. It's not Tim Burgess's laid-back drawl and loping, onstage-presence which captures my attention, however. No, it's keyboardist Rob Collins' Hammond organ sound, driving and insistent, which beats my ears into submission and has me transfixed. A couple of songs in and I'm completely hooked, dizzy and seduced by that distinctive, high-octane sound. Yet another Hammond casualty…

Back at home, I consult my teenage bibles, *Melody Maker* and *NME*, and discover, to my pleasure, that it is possible to trace a mini-modernist family tree from the bands The Charlatans cite as their influences. Groups such as Making Time and The Prisoners show up on my radar for the first time and start to open up a whole new world of musical possibilities.

Fast-forward a couple of years, and I become a Blow Up Club regular, freshly relocated from the Britpop Mecca of Camden's backstreets to Soho's infamous Wag Club, a venue soaked in its own brand of musical history. It was Blow Up which helped to really kick-start my appreciation of the 'scene'. Who wouldn't be seduced by the sight of London modernists dressed in their sharpest gear cutting a dash on the dance floor to tunes such a Ray Charles' 'I Don't Need No Doctor' and Benny Spellman's 'Fortune Teller'? My ears were opened to the finest quality '60s R&B, Northern Soul and Motown, and I couldn't get enough. A trip to Adam of London on Portobello Road saw me fitted with a three-button, tonic suit, blowing my savings in the process, but now at least I looked the part.

There was one crucial thing missing, however: wheels, and two of them. By now I was a student living off economy beans and 16p noodles, but I had my priorities straight: my first scooter, a white PX 125 disc model, purchased on finance and customised (or rather, bastardised, in retrospect) in a mod-by-numbers garb of lights and Union Jacks. It became my ticket into the local scooter club, allowing me to meet and mix with other like-minded members whom I now count as close friends.

The August Bank Holiday weekend of 2002 sees me, my PX 125 and several scooter club pals riding down to the Isle of Wight Scooter Rally. Setting off late, a decision is taken to spend the night at a camp site en route in Arundel. Arriving in the town, we waste no time in getting down to the serious business of sampling the local real ale. Hours later, we merrily fall out of the pub with full stomachs and empty wallets, but soon come to regret our indulgence as the heavens open, sending us dashing to clumsily set up our tents in the driving rain. At 6.30am, word goes round that campers who haven't checked in the night before will be asked to pay the next day. With all our money lining the pub's tills, we decide to make a quick getaway and, rain-battered and hung over, try to dismantle our tents as swiftly and silently as possible. We reach our parked scooters and, to avoid attracting attention, attempt to push them through the quagmire to the nearest exit, all the while desperately trying to stifle fits of laughter. Mud-spattered, we reach the gates, make a quick head count and start up our scooters. Behind us, the camp site owner, alerted by the sound of our engines, arrives at the gates, fist shaking, just in time to see us speed off into the distance.

Rob Parker.

CASUALS

Stuart Deabill, '80s Chelsea Casual.

Summer 1982, just left school and although I'd seen the odd person in what we now come to call Casual attire, it never hit me till the day a few of us went up to Ruislip Lido where some of the other kids from my manor Northolt were going for a row with some rockabilly/ted types.

As I got off the bus, amongst the Adidas kagoules/Tshirts and Levi's which most of us were sporting was this fella I vaguely knew from school. He looked resplendent in a navy/red/white cashmere diamond Pringle, what I later found out was faded Lois Jeans and light blue Adidas Gazelles. I couldn't take my eyes of the jumper, I never imagined something that possibly Bernard Gallagher or Nick Faldo would wear, would ever rock my world. He was even first in for the row so he became a cult hero in my eyes in an instant.

That was my introduction into the world of Casual as it later became known. I badgered my mum and dad something rotten for something similar, I'd already got a pair of Farah's to go with my new Adidas Hawaii's but the jumper was another world. Even back then it was 70–80 quid, but on holiday in Bournemouth we went into this big department store and there was Pringles in the August sale.

Happy Days!

With some birthday dough and the old man finally relenting with his wallet, I managed to purchase a plain light blue V Neck. That buzz of putting that jumper on with the Farah's and Hawaii's made me feel I was unique, special and I walked round the chalet park that night feeling untouchable. By the time the football season started, I realised quickly that I was just one of many who had the road to Damascus (Or Stuart's, W12) over the summer and all my mates had got on board.

As Chelsea were struggling in the second division at the time, the away days to Rotherham and Leeds became fashion parades not only to show the away fans the way forward dress-wise (the arrogance of being young and from London!) but also to show each other who had the latest items. It became far more important than the games itself as we were shocking on the pitch. I'd only just started work on the dreaded Youth Opportunity Scheme at £25 a week, and after bunging my mum some money was left with 15 notes.

As things were out of my league, you had to spend wisely. It helped that the local golf shops got broken into on a regular basis but a Fila BJ Velour track top was out of the question.

Then I started buying and selling records amongst other things so that helped to keep the wardrobe fresh. As 1982 went into 1983, the label of a certain tennis player, Sergio Tacchini, became a massive part of my young Casual life.

As I'd started to become a regular to Stuart's he would always drop a fiver off the retail price for me. I bought a white tracksuit with an almost waffle type material which was the most impressive item in my wardrobe. The name of the model escapes me but wearing that to Marcia Baillie's 18th party in Harrow cricket club I felt that I would be batting the women off with a shitty stick,

I felt that good. Especially as my hair was at the right length for me to flick out of my eye for added drama.

That was until my mate Phil pulled the bottoms down when I was holding 2 pints in front of everyone. Never again did I wear the bottoms out. As Chelsea had saved themselves from relegation at Bolton where I had managed to spill coffee on my new beige Diamond Lyle and Scott jumper on the train which made me feel like a tramp for the rest of the day, we all looked forward to the new season as Bates had pulled out some decent players and on the opening day we smashed Derby 5-0.

When I looked around me in the West Stand benches that afternoon, it seemed like every kid was wearing a label of some sort, apart from the few muggy boneheads still wearing MA1 jackets and DM's.

I'd bought some Lois Cords and split the hem to give them extra width over my new brand Diadora Borg Elite. The kangaroo leather made them feel like you were wearing gloves. Very handy if you had to avoid the police baton when needed (Newcastle springs to mind). Also the ubiquitous Kickers boot (or Noddy Boot) became a staple on the trotter front. The piece in *The Face* magazine that summer gave us the name Casual and it stuck. And Chelsea was Casual.

We had the swagger that the clothes gave you the confidence to carry as we strode purposely around alien streets. We had the team that had the swagger in abundance on the pitch for the first time since the early '70s and we turned out in droves at cities and towns such as Sheffield, Manchester, Blackburn and Derby. No one came near us that season on the pitch, on the terraces and on the clobber front. I loved every second of that season, getting back in the local to give it large after an arduous train journey home from some hick town and people asking you how much the Fila Mohair jumper you was styling was. (Though when my best mate bought an identical colour I nearly cried, such was the individualist in us true dressers. He never did it again).

The strive to be part of something but to be wearing something that no one else had was an unbelievably heady time to be young and alive. Chelsea got promoted and the first game of the new season was Arsenal away! We had the whole Clock End and to me it was the defining moment of being a teenage Chelsea Casual. 15,000 crammed into that end alone and most of those golden faces were under 25 and wearing Armani to YSL. When Kerry Dixon scored, the whole end with scores amongst scores of wedge haircuts, Lacoste and Fila Polo shirts and Fiorucci jean'd kids going absolutely barmy stays with me.

As the season went on the clothes got more garish and colourful and I remember an ill-thought out outfit of an overhead Leather 3 coloured patchwork jacket, pink Pringle polo and Canary yellow cords worn with grey Trimm Trabs. No wonder the old man thought I was on the turn.

As the '80s progressed, the style sort of left me (though I was still sporting Adidas Trainers and Lacoste) as I started getting involved in bands then in 1990 a certain Massimo Osti came into my life and carried me back in, but that's another story. Always wondered what happened to the kid in the Cashmere Pringle...

Stuart Deabill.

★ ★ ★

Paul Jobson, on 'a fairly unremarkable date in football history' that was in fact a significant day for him.

In the overall scheme of things, Saturday 4th December, 1982 is a fairly unremarkable date in football history but one that proved to be altogether more significant for me and my oldest friend – Andy.

After a morning spent playing football for the school in Leeds, a coach ride back to York found us landing at the War Memorial in readiness to catch the Pullman coach back to Leeds to watch the game against QPR Division 2 (as was).

Only there was no coach due to lack of numbers. By some sort of fluke, one of the other Leeds fans cadged us a lift in a works van which conveniently dropped us right outside of the ground in time for kick off. Where we found that the apathy about that day's game was not just confined to York-based Leeds fans, a paltry 11,528 (this was also in part to the Kop being closed as part of a two-game ban following crowd trouble a few weeks earlier against Newcastle when ball bearings fired from the crowd felled Kevin Keegan) watched Leeds lose a lack lustre game 1-0 to a team on their way to winning the championship and promotion to the 1st Division.

We walked back to Leeds Station, no doubt discussing the relative merits of whether or not Leeds were going to be able to mount a serious promotion challenge and re-gain their 1st Division status at the first attempt (they didn't, finishing a disappointing 8th after drawing too many games in the first season that 3 points for a win were introduced). Whilst waiting on the station concourse, we were witness to a brief skirmish involving rival fans. Not an unusual occurrence at that time. After police intervention, I noticed that Andy had independently discreetly covered his scarf whilst I had removed mine and shoved it into my pocket. Neither of us mentioned what we'd both covered our colours because we didn't want to admit that we'd both been shitting it. It was the last time either of us ever wore our colours to a game…

Once on the safe haven of the train and with our fear subsiding, we started to chat about what we'd just seen, lads our age, wearing no colours, looking so smart and dressing differently to anything we'd ever seen in the village north of York, where we were growing up. We marvelled how lads similar to our age could be so carefree, cocksure, fearless and together as they swaggered off the station concourse. They seemed to bounce as they walked, head up and flicking to get fringes out of their faces, eye contact, shoulders back, cagoules hanging off their shoulders. To two naïve 15 year olds, it looked exciting, exhilarating and fun!

Leeds' promotion challenge continued to falter, to be honest, it never really got going! The Pullman coaches were cancelled on a regular basis meaning me and Andy travelled to games more and more on the train. We discovered to our amazement that there were also lads from York who were like and dressed the same as those we'd seen at Leeds Station and not only that, we recognised some of them from being in the years above us at school. Soon, some of them would strike up a conversation asking us about what we thought about the game, in turn we would probe and ask questions about the clothes they wore and where we could get them. Some answered honestly whilst others bullshit us that they'd been to Manchester or London and there was only so many made blah blah blah. These chats were on the train journey only as once at Leeds, the older lads went in search of pubs; we instead would wander around the centre, before finding a chippy then making our way to Elland Road.

Andy and me were desperate to start looking like the lads at the match; we both worked on the same milk round and had been feverishly saving. We ventured into York to each buy some trainers. At the time, Adidas Samba seemed to be a popular choice with the lads at the match, Andy played safe and that's what he bought. I walked into the shop with my full intention of doing the same but saw a similar looking trainer for a lot less – Adidas Kick. No doubt seduced by the saving then allowing me to also buy a LP of some description, I went for those, big mistake! Adidas Kick it turned out weren't considered a trainer to be seen in nor were they sufficiently unusual for me to try and bluff about their rarity. They weren't worn many times before being 'retired', later to be put to good use for playing 5-a-side. I started to save to buy a different pair of trainers with the added grief of explaining to my mum why I was intending to buy some more new trainers again despite the other ones being brand new and 'having plenty of wear left in them'. Second time around, I went for some Adidas Monaco that seemed to avoid too much stick.

Our rite of passage in both life and going to the match continued. Pubs started to become within our reach as we grew up and older. Probably like most young, underage drinkers, we gravitated to those pubs that had a reputation for not checking ages and being easy to get served in. Dropping into conversations with the older lads on the train that we'd been out on the town the night before and where we'd been, we recoiled when the older lads scoffed at where we'd been, imparting advice and wisdom on which were 'the pubs to go to'. We'd then go in search of these the following week to see if we could get in and served. Mostly these visits would end in disappointment for either being refused entry – more often than not for wearing trainers rather than us being underage, or that none of the other match lads were in there. Eventually through us leaving as others arrived or us arriving as they left, we worked out there was a routine and timing was everything.

Again we gravitated towards the older lads we recognised from our school, who by now didn't seem too embarrassed to be associated with us. Andy and me were studying our A Levels so our friendships typically remained within a close circle of those people we either lived near or went to school with. Friends who'd left school at 16 for apprenticeships and YTS Schemes had branched out, widening their circle of friends from all over York. School rivalries a thing of the past.

Familiarity from the match and on the pub circuit would slowly result in nods of acknowledgement and snatched conversations whilst waiting to be served, chats usually around football, music and clothes. The older lads from school would fill in the gaps in terms of who was who, who was alright, who was better for knowing and who should be given a wide berth.

There was a hierarchy of respect based on all manner of things – dress sense, music knowledge, sporting prowess (typically football, boxing or both), fighting ability, how game lads were and notoriety for all manner of things illegal. Beer was the universal 'drug of choice', any other drug use was confined to a limited few who occasionally smoked spliffs, took wraps of speed but heroin was slowly getting a grip on a very small minority who typically would then disappear from this social scene.

I remained big into music and regularly would have my personal stereo headphones round my neck on a night out having been listening to music as I walked into town. This drew the attention from one of the 'top lads' – Gary, who was about 24/25 whereas I was 17/18. To me, 24/25 seemed ancient! He asked me what I was listening to and I produced from my pockets one or two C90 cassettes with whatever I had taped at that time – probably New Order or something similarly 'indie'.

Gary knew everyone, was massively into his music and one of the best and innovative dressers in the York scene. He'd regularly rock up wearing something – shoes (Clarks or Hush Puppies) or Hiking boots rather than trainers, Hiking/Mountaineering clothing instead of jeans, a chunky knit jumper, looking scruffy when everyone was going smart etc., be roundly ridiculed then invariably as other lads noticed others at the match wearing the same, they would seek to emulate them and Gary. You'd then see him flogging the gear that weeks before he was having the mickey taken out of, often to the most vocal piss takers then funding whatever next he wanted to buy, the same cycle seemed to happen over and over again. There was a desire to be seen in something different, to be innovative and to wear stuff that people were complimentary about or copied. You got dog's abuse if you were busted for copying someone or alternatively wore something that was also worn by someone not considered to have a clue about their dress sense. It was good-natured one-upmanship.

A few weeks later, Gary approached me and handed over a

cassette he'd done, loads of Northern Soul, rare groove, reggae, funk and hip hop. All stuff I'd never heard. It was a nice touch and put me on to loads of stuff I probably wouldn't have known about or got into.

I stayed in touch with Gary when I moved to Manchester to go to the Polytechnic and he and a few others would come across for gigs. Around that time, we went to see The Farm, Run DMC, Trouble Funk, Public Enemy, LL Cool J, Eric B & Rakim and Derek B amongst others.

Good memories and a great time to come of age!

Paul Jobson.

★ ★ ★

'A Casual State of Mind'
by Derek Nicklin

The first real scene that hit home with a defined dress code for me was Two Tone and Mod around 1978. I had just left school and was working so I had a bit of disposable income to hand. Really I was more Rude Boy than Mod. So for me it was more tonic suits, Fred Perry polo shirts, tassled loafers and even a pork pie hat. With the exception of the Fred Perry essential polo shirt, a lot of it was pretty cheap and nasty looking back on it. For example, tonic suits for £29.99 from Oasis market or Nelson House in Birmingham.

Shopping at that time began to get dangerous too, with a mixture of punks, skins, mods and rude boys all populating the city centre and looking for a 'wet behind the ears country boy from the sticks' and robbing your purchases or just generally giving you grief a regular occurrence (that was soon to be taken to another level).

Living in the backwaters of Worcestershire & being Albion meant I/we weren't the sharpest to get it, I'm afraid. Looking back the first obviously different dressers were Liverpool/Everton & I can remember going to Goodison Park, season 1980, & to say we stood out like sore thumbs is an understatement! Straight (at the time quite tight) jeans, seemingly everyone in Adidas Samba or Kick, anoraks & everyone seemed to sport a wedge/ flick hairstyle. We in our defence, knew no different & were still in cross-over late mod/two tone, MA1 flight jackets etc… it made for an interesting afternoon, to say the least!!

I know plenty don't/won't agree but the big explosion came with sportswear and that meant London! Spurs came to Albion in one of the last games of season 1983 & I was mesmerised by the colours, strange logos, split jeans, I JUST HAD TO HAVE IT!!!!

Discovered that 10 minutes up the road there was a specialist racket shop (Hagley Sports) that sold Fila, Tacchini, 1881, Ellesse & I never looked back!

The tale that to me shows just how the scene mushroomed in months was that summer, had my first "shopping trip" to London as I though it "must" be the only place you could get it from, Olympus, 303 Oxford St, Tacchini Dallas £60 (close on 3 weeks wages) a Lacoste roll-neck & Pringle diamond, I thought I was King Shit! Another couple of additions & first game of following season was the plum Villa away, meet set up for The Shakesphere on the morning & I donned the full Sergio with Nike Wimbledon thinking I'd be untouchable (at least in the clothing stakes) only to find half a dozen in the same Dallas & out of nowhere WE WERE ALL CASUALS!! Here the story begins!

After that Spurs game I discovered we actually had a specialist racquet shop in Worcester and one in Hagley just over 15 miles away, so I discovered what those funny logos were and the prices. I suppose my first purchase Casual-wise was a red Pringle v neck from the local golf club pro shop, weighed in at something like £29.99 and I remember me dad saying I was off my head paying that much. I don't mind admitting it then became all encompassing & the culture literally took over my life.

The thing that was so obvious to me was that the average Joe in the street didn't have a clue, yeah they could lump everyone in the "football hooligan" bracket but to do so was to miss the point and the scene was so much more than just football. I will add however that the two were inexplicably linked, once into it was easy to see where some of the early influences came from, while I'm not dismissing Merseyside at all and fully respect that they were the first in my opinion that dressed 'differently', the whole 'who was first?' debate bores me to death.

I naturally gravitated down towards London & sportswear (and that WAS the look that the scene as a whole adorned), Farah slacks, croc shoes, gold rope chains etc, didn't pay it much attention but this had been the staple attire for West Indian fellas around the reggae scene, perhaps the forerunners?

It also was so much a case of what you wore, how you wore it, chaps just looked so good and smart and, if we're honest, we all walked (or tried to) with a certain swagger in those formative years it was so fast moving, items literally had shelf lives of weeks/days in some cases, keep up or face ridicule so things were sold on, passed down, swopped anything to try and keep it and look fresh. Then there was the trouble, but enough has been written about that!!!

Derek Nicklin.

GREBO

Si Sharp, on how history is flawed if it is always be written by the 'winners'.

"U2", I ventured with hesitation. John Adams, the cool kid, eyed me up and down. "Hmmm, that'll do" he replied. It was 1989 and I had started at a new school. John had lined us all up and asked us in turn who our favourite bands were. Obviously my answer wasn't very good, but it seemed my friend Nick and I had enough potential for John to take us under his wing and introduce us to a new world. John was a grebo.

We were indoctrinated into a world of hanging out, drinking cider, undercuts, smoking cigarettes, girls with dreadlocks, and new exciting music. We embraced it all but for Nick and me, more so than for John as it transpired, it was all about the music and the bands. Bands that were, needless to say, a shitload better than U2.

Seemingly every other weekend we'd be getting the train into London, or somewhere more far-flung to go see Pop Will Eat Itself or Senseless Things or whoever it might be. In our village Nick and I were solitary figures in our combat trousers, Doc Martens (with band logos painted on), long sleeve band t-shirts, hair long on top, and shaved up the back and sides. But once we were on that train we'd find instant company amongst the other kids easily identifiable from their tour t-shirts, although importantly never the t-shirt of the band you were going to see that night – that was an unspoken rule.

We met so many people that way that I'm still in touch with today, Simon and Phil, two brothers on the train to Kilburn for a Ned's Atomic Dustbin gig; Matt, in his much admired PWEI/ Pepsi t-shirt; Diana, the girl who offered us biscuits outside a Mega City Four gig and then got us in for free.

What was it about the music that was so inspiring? Some of it was the allure of the alternative. You couldn't hear these bands on the radio – you'd find out about them on mix-tapes or older siblings' record collections. The UK bands I've mentioned along with all the American bands (Mudhoney, Dinosaur Jr, Sonic Youth) from their (still underground) alternative rock scene. A big part of it was that these guys were accessible. They weren't aloof rock-gods playing stadiums beyond a wall of beefed-up security- they were just ordinary people, dressing like us, reading the same comics, replying to our letters and tolerating our stage-diving at small-to-medium venues around the country. They had a disdain for the rock 'n' roll lifestyle myth which they'd learnt from punk and new wave, but were also cultural magpies dropping *Blade Runner* and *Aliens* samples into their music. The whole scene felt so perfectly of its time but utterly apart from the status quo. The scene wasn't political in nature, but when you're at home in a subculture, then political protest isn't a very big step, so some joined the traveller movement.

All the bands shared that attitude that they were living in the present, looking forward and were in it for the music with no desire to compromise in order to make money. Some expressed that by embracing technology and mashing up genres like PWEI,

Jesus Jones or Gaye Bykers on Acid, some like Mega City Four through their lyrics and desire to reach every corner of the country. It was often derisively claimed at the time that all the bands used to sell more t-shirts than they did records, and there was clearly something in that. My dad used to mock me for providing the bands with free advertising, but those t-shirts were a way of us fans communicating with each other, assessing each others' level of commitment to our hobby and, hell, we thought we looked pretty cool.

With hindsight it was a pretty short-lived scene. Most the bands peaked creatively in 1989-90 and commercially a couple of years after. The US alternative rock movement slowly started to overshadow it after Nirvana broke through. However it was Suede's *Melody Maker* cover in 1993 that spelled the end as it paved the way for the Britpop invasion – re-introducing the 'man on the street' to guitar music, leaving grebo running on fumes until its unofficial swansong – The Wonder Stuff's (then) final gig at the Phoenix Festival in the summer of 1994.

History is written by the winners, so now the accepted version of the '90s jumps from acid house to grunge via Madchester with barely a mention of these bands and the scene, but you know what – that's fine. I can think of nothing less appropriate than Carter The Unstoppable Sex Machine being inducted into the Rock n Roll Hall of Fame. It feels now like an anomaly, the music and the scene doesn't seem to fit with the narrative of UK guitar music and its neat line that starts at The Smiths and ends up at Coldplay via the Stone Roses and Oasis. Grebo was a weirdly scruffy blip on the cardiograph flatline of indie music, an explosion of subcultural energy which, for all of its popularity, Britpop's return to traditional songwriting, national pride and anthemic choruses lacked.

Compared to now when anything new or 'alternative' is immediately co-opted by the taste-makers before being groomed for commercial success, we were one of the last youth tribes to congregate around a sound largely unnoticed by marketing departments and advertising agencies. We owned our favourite bands and that personal investment in music has never left me. You'll find ex-grebo's out there, going to gigs, promoting nights, writing about music, and organising festivals. We look different and we've moved on because that was the whole point.

I may have thrown myself into different genres afterwards before growing up and settling down but I still have a healthy distrust of the mainstream and an irreverence for the past, and these were things I learnt in the moshpits of the Astoria, the Mean Fiddler and numerous other venues around the UK.

That said, I had a great time so if you'll indulge me a bit of nostalgia - there's a memory that has survived despite all the effort I've made to destroy braincells. A girl at that Wonder Stuff gig at the Phoenix wearing a homemade t-shirt with a lyric from 'Piece of Sky' from their *Hup!* album: "It'll never be the same, but we're not to blame". I don't think it really meant anything beyond acknowledging the finality of the actual event but it stayed with me – it's rare that life grants you an actual subtitle, an obvious and literal piece of narration to help make sense of everything.

Si Sharp.

★ ★ ★

Martin Roach, from the Introduction to the 2005 Re-issue of his book, The Eight Legged Atomic Dustbin Will Eat Itself.

All roads lead to Stourbridge. Or at least, they did when I was a kid. The 555 bus took me there from my home in Kingswinford, along the main road and on to the Midlands' equivalent of the Westway, Stourbridge Ring Road. Maybe not quite as mystical as Joe Strummer's west London thoroughfare, and certainly not as famous, but there you go. Any kids caught graffiti-ing underpass walls in Stourbridge while wearing boiler suits would get a swift, sharp slap round the chops from their old man, rather than a feature in *i-D*.

Stourbridge town centre is an island in the middle of a multi-lane ring road, so it's not exactly a popular spot for ramblers. The bus would drop me off opposite the Crystal Leisure Centre – complete with 'space-age' water slide, which ran outside the actual building (it's a Tesco now) – from where I would walk along a small road and up the side of a pub called The Mitre, on my way to college.

It was 1985 and The Smiths were just about the most important band in the country. Goths slithered around Stourbridge's side streets, but a lot of students went to a nightclub called Tweedies in the High Street to listen to Simple Minds and U2. Robert Plant lived near Stourbridge and occasionally you saw him in the town; Slade, Wizzard and Diamond Head were fellow locals, but the polluted environs of Birmingham might as well have been a thousand miles away. London? Camden? Where?

But something was festering in those back streets – unbeknown to me, something that would alter my world forever. It was the genesis of three bands: Pop Will Eat Itself, The Wonder Stuff and Ned's Atomic Dustbin. The most important three bands in my life. In June of 1986, PWEI released the crude yet brilliant 'Poppies Say Grrr!!!' and, like a time-delayed bomb that had been set, my future had been infected… and as yet I didn't even know it.

The scene switches to Safeway's in Kingswinford some time later. The cheese aisle. Miles Hunt, bedraggled and long-haired lead singer of The Wonder Stuff appears to be selecting a mild cheddar – according to my mom, who was watching in bemusement from across the fruit and veg. Behind a pyramid of own-brand beans, a gaggle of girls are chatting nervously. "That's him, it is, it is!!" Mom came straight home and told me, "You ought to write a book about him and his band."

So I did.

By then, of course, PWEI and The Wonder Stuff were well established on the national music radar. For anyone living around Stourbridge they were virtual veterans. Then my sister Joanne walked in to our front room (you don't have sitting or drawing rooms in the West Midlands, only fronts), which I was helping to decorate. "Listen to this, it's Ned's Atomic Dustbin and it's called 'Grey Cell Green'."

Bingo. Another chapter.

At the time, I was working selling suits to old men smelling of urine and tobacco for a firm called George Arthur Dunn. They've gone now. The shops. And, I suppose, most of those old men.

The day after my mom told me about Miles buying cheese, I gave up my job. I had a powerful Amstrad word-processor – 64K, I believe – and started writing the next morning. I didn't need to research a lot, it was like saying, "How do you get to Stourbridge town centre?" I didn't need to speak to "their people, who'd touch-base with my people". I knew Jonn Penney of Ned's Atomic Dustbin drank in The Mitre, so I made myself known. Without hesitating he agreed to be interviewed. To this day I don't know why, other than because he is a thoroughly decent chap. I had no writing experience, no magazine behind me, no publishing deal, no money and essentially no hope. But he said yes. I shall always be eternally grateful to him for that.

I vividly remember sitting in his house in Cemetery Road, Lye and finding myself amazed that he brought in a plate of custard creams. They were normal ones too, not posh stuff. He was a pop star, but he even made his own tea.

We chatted and then he said he'd call Clint Mansell of Pop

Will Eat Itself. He did, Clint agreed to speak too and even wrote an introduction for my book, although not before he berated me for being a 'fucking lightweight' – simply because he hadn't seen me in The Talbot before. I remember vividly walking down Stourbridge High Street with him, this alien creature loping along, six-foot-plus with towering red dreadlocks. He probably didn't notice, but everyone was looking at him. I felt like I was caught in the middle of Stourbridge's own Roswell Incident.

The book that I wrote had virtually no musical context, no analysis of where grebo fitted into the greater scheme of music history. That's precisely because – like so many grebos – I didn't know and frankly didn't really care. I lived in Stourbridge, the three best bands in the country came from Stourbridge, what else was there to know? I just wanted an overview, a sense of why and how this odd little phenomenon had created itself.

Pretty soon, I had a good, solid fifteen rejection letters from publishers barely able to hide their disbelief that anyone might want to read – let alone invest money – in a book about three bands no one in their publishing circles had ever heard of. One even wrote, "PS: Do you know anything about Michael Jackson?" (I didn't.)

All I had to do now was get The Wonder Stuff involved – who, at the turn of the '80s into the '90s, were the most commercially successful of the three acts. I wrote a letter and drove all the way to Redditch, along its silent, smooth tarmac veins and to the door of Les Johnson, the band's manager. I'd never met a band manager before, so I expected drugs and groupies. Les was in his slippers.

He promised to put the idea to the band.

He did.

They said, "No."

I was gutted.

I wrote my book anyway.

For ten weeks I wrote every day, speaking along the way to various key players in the story. Finally, with the rejection pile standing at 32 letters, the manuscript was ready. For some odd reason I don't recall, I phoned a calendar maker in Halesowen (near Stourbridge), who thought I was insane but printed up a thousand shiny blue copies even so, costing £3.50 each. I took the cover's lurid pink and blue colours from an old box of 'Fuzzy Felts'. I chose those colours because it looked like the letters wobbled when you shook the top.

Then I did what any self-respecting fan of those bands did on a Saturday – I went to an indie record shop. The first one was Mike Lloyd Megastores in Wolverhampton. He took fifty despite the lack of a bar code ("A what?"). I got on the bus and arrived home two hours later, to find a message saying he needed fifty more, as twenty-five had already sold.

It had started.

This was what grebo was capable of.

I bought a National Express coach ticket and travelled the UK. In each town I would go first to the library, photocopy the Yellow Pages music-shops section and then hit the pavement. I sold them firm sale, cash up front and I couldn't print them fast enough. The first thousand went within a month. Okay, I was only charging £3.50 trade price, thus making a profit of £0.00. But something was happening, I could feel it.

Another thousand were printed in blue. Yet more indie record-shop visits. I also sold them outside gigs, by those three bands and by other acts like the brilliant Mega City Four and the Senseless Things. They were nearly sold out again when I walked into the Virgin Megastore in Nottingham. The man behind the counter said, "Thank God, we've had all sorts of fucking weirdos in here after this. Give me a hundred and phone this number." I did, it was head office and they ordered a thousand. I needed another reprint, a bar code and an ISBN, apparently (A what?). Virgin Megastores sent the red third edition into their shops and it became their fastest selling music book of the year. I was no fucking businessman, let me tell you that, but I knew that Virgin paid £3.50 and it cost me a few pence less than that to print it. My publishing label, Independent Music Press, was born.

One night I came home to find an answer-phone message from Miles Hunt: "Do you fancy doing a big interview for the new edition of your book?... and can we blag it for our fanclub magazine?" I did, they did and a new chapter wrote itself.

I sold nearly three thousand copies in indie and high-street record shops before I walked into a solitary bookshop. I never went into bookshops, neither did grebos.

I tell you this tale not because it is central to the story of these three bands or indeed, for that matter, the story of grebo – it isn't. Please forgive me the indulgence of reminiscence. It is to make a point. I tell you because it demonstrates the unique and quite staggering hold the groups all had on the psyche of a certain rather whiffy corner of the nation's youth during those fantastic years. They certainly had a hold on me, I worked my bollocks off for three years for bugger-all money but I never once considered calling it quits, those bands meant too much to me. But I wasn't alone, not by a long chalk. There were thousands of us.

Maybe it was because I was born in Stourbridge that I felt so moved by these three groups, but the story of that little book and its colossal impact on my life is directly related to the incredible success of and personalities in these bands. When I heard all three were re-forming, I couldn't resist catching up with a few old friends and seeing what they have been up to. You'd never believe what they'd been doing. Film scoring, being presidents of major record labels, DJ-ing to thousands of people, writing soundtracks for global television shows... oh yes, grebos are among you and you don't even realise it.

I tell you what, I will never be a fiction writer, but I can write about some strange and wonderful creatures: The Bass Thing. Dan Dan The Fast Drumming Man. Clint. Rat. Milo. Grebos. And there is one crucial point...

You couldn't make it up.

Lunatic magnets, modern idiots, my cure for sanity.

Martin Roach.

★ ★ ★

Dave, flying the flag for grebos.

Grebo was perhaps the ultimate insular 'scene' (not that any real grebo called it a scene). A lot of grebos I knew didn't really listen to much else other than the bands tagged with that name – PWEI, The Wonder Stuff, Ned's Atomic Dustbin, Carter USM, Mega City 4, Senseless Things et al. I listened to all of these bands and a few others and was fiercely proud and defensive of them. I remember in Martin Roach's *Eight Legged* book, PWEI's lead singer Clint Mansell did an Introduction about the 'scene' in which he said first and foremost there was 'no scene'. That's a classic grebo comment.

Not for grebo the meticulous and refined fashion of Mod or Two Tone; however, there was a style and a fashion, regardless of how unkempt it appeared. The T-shirts were a BIG thing. They were literally thousands of walking advertising boards and I don't think grebo usually gets enough credit for what – in my opinion – transformed modern band merchandising. Some grebos would never wear a band shirt to the actual gig by that group, but others wore whatever. I had a particular soft spot for Ned's Atomic Dustbin; their artwork, created by singer Jonn Penney's girlfriend Helga, was, for me, just amazing. I collected the shirts as much as I did the 12-inch and 45 releases. My absolute favourite was a long sleeve 'Kill Your Television' shirt, which had a black logo on a black top. I wore that thing till it started to fall apart but now, years later, it's safely enshrined in a box in the loft. I can't imagine what my grandkids will say when I pull that out to show them at

Xmas in the distant future, and explain the title! I still think the Ned's logo is one of the greatest band logos of all time.

Dr. Martens were the footwear of choice for any grebo, worn open, often flapping around the ankle. They'd often come off in the mosh pit and then you'd have a bastard of a job finding your pair after the show. Sometimes there'd be band logos painted on the boots, too. Rat from the Ned's always sported a pair of Dr. Martens. He was big into T-shirts also. My favourite shirt that he wore simply said, 'F★★kin' F★★k'.

When the big three grebo bands – PWEI, Stuffies and Neds – started to really enjoy success (festival headline slots, big albums, etc, don't forget) there was such an intense pride among grebos. Those bands were all accessible, decent lads and the feeling that they were 'normal' people who just happened to be in brilliant bands was cherished. I went to Reading Festival in 1991 when Ned's were second on the bill to the Sisters of Mercy, Carter were second on to James and PWEI were third on behind Iggy Pop and Sonic Youth (Kingmaker and Senseless Things were also on the main stage bill). The day grebo took over, in my opinion.

Tell you what though, some of the grebo haircuts were a sight! Massive floppy fringes, often shaved and undercut at the sides. Again, Ned's led the way with some of the most extreme versions of this and their fans soon followed suit. When they appeared on *Top of the Pops* with their single 'Happy' (a MASSIVE moment for grebos everywhere), the presenter made a smart-arse comment about their haircuts, like a band on the telly was supposed to have some kind of smart short, back and sides.

I'm in my 40s now and with kids and a mortgage, so those heady days going to festivals and sweaty gigs at JB's and other West Midlands venues seem a long way off. But when I put a Ned's tune on, I am suddenly transported back to that moment in my life. It is literally a time-machine; music that has really affected and influenced you has that ability. I still get a tingle down the spine when I play 'Happy' or one of the Ned's earlier

EPs, such as 'Grey Cell Green'. In that sense, the grebo is frozen in time, and will always be there – one of the most 'unfashionable', under-rated and under-valued of all the UK tribes. I know much of music history is written by trendy scribes who look down their noses at grebo, and for that reason many of the books and magazines have often airbrushed the grebo's part in British youth culture, at times almost out of existence. Do not be mislead. For a period (all too brief sadly), grebo *mattered* and that fact can never be denied.

Dave.

GLAM

Richard Carman, our 'solitary' glam fan.

I couldn't tell you what I did for most of that day, except that I was twelve years old and would have been at school, because I know for a fact it was a Thursday. Maybe I had a maths lesson, did some PE, running around the gym with shorts too short and hair too long. I probably had instant mashed potato as part of the school dinner, and walked home through the estate with Paul Montgomery in the warmth of a quiet summer afternoon. I couldn't tell you what I had for tea, or what was on the news. But I know what I did next. I watched *Top of the Pops*.

It was July 8th, 1972.

We all watched *Top of the Pops*. We all loved pop music. But The Beatles had grown up and moved away, and I had three LPs in the house, left behind by my older sister. *Ummagumma* by Pink Floyd, Dylan's *Nashville Skyline,* and Leonard Cohen's first album were pretty cool records to know inside out at the age of twelve, but they were my sister's music, and I had nothing yet to call my own.

And then he appeared. A twelve-string guitar, an odd, faltering

little tune, with a whimsical, "la-la-la" opening. And then…
BLOODY HELL!

David Bowie knocked us sideways. 'Starman' had more hooks than the Old Trafford dressing room: part Judy Garland, part Supremes. It's an irresistible record. But it was Dave himself – and don't ever call him "Dave" – who blew us away. The knowing grin, the fabulous haircut, the pencil thin legs, the ashed-out eyes, the tight little jump suit (we only had black and white TV, so we didn't know what colour it was), the boots, the band…

It never struck me as camp when he put his arm round Mick. I didn't really know what camp was. I was a hormonal twelve-year old in the north of England, and I had no idea of blurred sexuality, only of our blurred telly. But that night changed my life.

Fashions had been changing since the turn of the decade, and we all already wore the huge rounded collars, the tank-tops, and stacked-heel shoes with platform soles. We already had our hair cut into wedgy shapes, but we all had side-burns and our hair routinely covered our ears. Then came Dave.

The following day the classroom was split. "Did you see that bloke on *Top of the Pops* last night?"You either got it immediately, or hated it. And I loved it. "Something" had begun, and its name was Glam. Suddenly, post-Bowie the visual element of pop music was as important as the sound. If you got both right, it was fabulous. If you got one element wrong it could be awful. But great records mixed up with a great look completed the third great stride in pop music history. First there was Elvis, then there was The Beatles, then there was Bowie. Slade were funny, had ridiculous outfits, but made fabulous rock and roll records. Sweet looked like brickies who had found Bowie's stage gear and put it on in the dark, but had some ace records. Plenty of people would claim Bolan had kicked it all off, but T Rex still had a little air of whimsical '60s about them, but they were such exciting records. And then there were the older acts joining in – Gary

Glitter, Showaddywaddy, Mud, Alvin Stardust (Ziggy's cousin?). Even The Stones went glam, and Keith still covers himself in scarves and make-up.

That summer we went on holiday to Scotland. In a camp site in Crieff there was a disco. They played 'Starman' and Alice Cooper's 'School's Out' all night. Nothing else. It was bliss. The girls were gorgeous, the blokes were clumsy, the jeans were flared and the make-up was everywhere. I was still wearing jumpers my mum knitted for me, but in my head all I had were David Bowie songs.

And then we came home and there was a second punch… Roxy Music. 'Virginia Plain' was an awesome debut. Bryan Ferry was SOOOOOOOO cool. Even though his feel was more '50s, Ferry had the same intelligence as Bowie, the same articulate playing with the genre, the same air of decadent knowingness. And, where Bowie had Ronson as a foil ("if you didn't like Paul you could always like John"), Roxy had Eno.

The thing that the media forget about glam now – and I guess most pop movements – is that this was aimed at kids from eleven to fourteen. The lower ranked bands appeared on *Crackerjack* and *Blue Peter*. It was lovely. For me it was always about Bowie, and then Lou Reed, The Stooges, Bolan. *Aladdin Sane* followed *Ziggy*, and remains my favourite album of the era. But Dave was moving on. *Pin-Ups* had the same debauched swagger, but by 1974 it was gone. 'Rebel Rebel' was the last real glam single. Bowie got into soul (divinely), Eno left Roxy and Ferry donned a tuxedo and started making smoochie dance tracks for the girls, while in my opinion Bolan lost his way. A lot of the second division acts carried on ploughing a furrow that now looked increasingly bare. When Bowie moved, we went with him. Getting sick of disco and tat, a bunch of Bowie fans dyed their hair red again, spiked it up, slapped on some make-up and invented punk. It was ace – we were all ready for it.

They were the happiest of days. Nearly thirty years later I

met David Bowie. I got a chance to chat for a few minutes. I called him "Dave." I have never forgiven myself.

Richard Carman.

GOTH

*Pete Scathe, widely acknowledged
Goth expert and historian, with a very
personal view.*

When the goth scene started in the late '70s and early '80s I was a teenager, living in Portsmouth, on the south coast. Portsmouth certainly wasn't at the centre of things, but it had its own alternative club (Grannies) and was on the gig circuit, so a fair few goth bands played there, including Sex Gang Children, Alien Sex Fiend, The March Violets (twice!) and the Sisters of Mercy.

It was also close enough to London for me to go up and see bands there, although it was usually a choice between missing the last song or the last bus.

I initially became aware of goth bands via John Peel's late night radio show, which was vitally important for breaking new music at the time. I was into "alternative" bands in general, and goth bands were part of a wider scene that involved bands such as Joy Division, early New Order, Fad Gadget, Killing Joke, The Chameleons, The Birthday Party, Cocteau Twins, 1919, Rudimentary Peni and so on. Bands such as UK Decay, Danse Society, Xmal Deutchsland and Play Dead fitted perfectly into this wider post-punk scene, and at no time did I ever care about whether bands were "goth" or not. It just happened that a lot of the bands I liked were bands who would later get tagged "goth". These bands also had an effect on my wardrobe – I shifted from a general post-punk/alternative look to a "goth" look, where it helped that being skinny was a positive advantage, and that a high-maintenance goth mohawk added about six inches to my height (many drunken goths had long conversations with the top of my mohawk).

I also liked the androgynous side of the early goth scene, which was one of the things that marked it out from the early '80s punk scene. It was usually easy to tell punk men and girls apart, but not always that easy with goths – I was once standing beside one of my male friends who was wearing a wedding dress when one of his friends walked up to him, complimented him on his wedding dress, pointed at me and said, "Is that your new girlfriend?".

There were downsides of course – I once went to a pub with a large group of people and the barman pointed at me and said "I'm happy to serve the rest of you but I'm not serving that". And you had to be wary of certain Casuals, Punks, Skinheads and/ or Psychobillies with a penchant for Goth-bashing (especially if you'd accidentally slept with their girlfriend).

But for someone like me who was small, slim and decidedly un-macho, the goth scene was brilliant. It was no doubt brilliant for gay and bisexual people too, although I don't remember nearly as many gay/bi people as you might expect (despite outsiders often assuming all goth blokes were gay). And one huge advantage for me was that quite a few goth girls seemed to find this weird little bloke with spiky hair and make-up curiously attractive.

So from my point of view the goth scene was a total godsend. In fact if God had sat down and thought to himself, *It's about time I sorted out a scene for this Pete chap*, he probably couldn't have done a much better job.

The early goth scene was nothing like the later cliché of lonely goths moping in their bedrooms it was vibrant, exciting, fun, and based around following excellent live bands. Early goth gigs were lively events, and the usual dancing style was chicken dancing, which involved flailing elbows (the decidedly more sedate Gothic Two Step, where goths in flowing dresses walked back and forth on the dancefloor to the Sisters of Mercy amidst billowing clouds of smoke was a much later invention that I first encountered in Leeds in the mid-80s, my first thought being "Why are these people walking on the dancefloor?").

Then, some time around 1985, things seemed to be changing, and not in a good way from my point of view. I remember going to a Cult gig around 84/85 and noticing that the support band (Balaam And The Angel) had suspiciously long hair. Shortly after this the Sisters of Mercy started playing Led Zeppelin as their warm-up music, another ominous sign.

As well as this, most of my favourite bands started splitting up or going in directions I wasn't keen on. Bands had split up before – UK Decay, Ritual, Bauhaus – but there always seemed to be something new coming along to take their place, and this time that wasn't happening. Instead, the few new bands that were emerging seemed to be "goth rock" bands like The Mission and Fields of the Nephilim. And older bands either went in a rock direction or seemed to be aiming for failed pop careers, sometimes under the malevolent misguidance of major record companies (or at least that's how I saw it at the time).

The goth scene carried on, and in fact was probably more popular than ever in the mid-80s, but it wasn't the same. The early bands had seemed to be doing something new and exciting, but somehow the punk-post-punk-goth musical trajectory that had led away from stale old rock had come around full circle, and we were back with stale old rock again.

This really hit home when I was listening to an "alternative" radio show in 1987 and was wondering why they were playing what sounded to me like AC/DC. Then I suddenly recognised the voice as Ian Astbury, and realised it was in fact The Cult.

At the same time, fashion and hairstyles had gone in a rock/ hippy direction, and voluminous clothes and patchouli oil were suddenly everywhere. And the scene, like all scenes, had acquired rules, things that people thought they had to do to "fit in" properly. In the case of the goth scene, the very fact that the scene had been called "goth" led to some daft attempts to be "gother than thou" which could lead to people trying to be deep, dark and mysterious, and spending far too much time in graveyards. Or even to reading original "gothic" literature – I once accidentally got a small tranche of goths hooked on Thomas Love Peacock (I'm still not sure if they realised he was writing satire). This caused much bemusement to me and much amusement to the media, for whom goth had become a very easy target.

I carried on with the goth scene even though towards the end of the '80s goth seemed to be in terminal decline in Portsmouth – the goth scene still seemed strong in London with clubs like Wraith and Slimelight, but even there the scene was kept artificially alive by a steady influx of foreign goths.

But somehow goth carried on, despite the dwindling numbers. The internet helped goths keep in contact, like some sort of endangered species self-help forum. And after a "goth holiday" in the early '90s I got interested in the scene again, even opening a goth night, Resurgence (which I still run occasionally, as well as a goth/fetish night, Pandemonia). So when in the late '90s Marilyn Manson fans and metallers started to appropriate the goth look and people started thinking "goth" and "metal" were somehow the same thing, I thought I'd better enlighten people about what goth was and where it came from. Which is how I wrote what turned out to be the first in-depth online history of goth: www. historyofgoth.com.

Pete Scathe.

★ ★ ★

Natasha Scharf, acclaimed author and Goth expert, on her own Goth beginnings.

I remember a friend of mine once joking that every village has at least three goths and they always congregate by the local war memorial. My own early experiences of being a goth were somewhat different as I didn't know any other people who were into the same music or style of clothing as me – I used to get bullied at school for looking different. But a few months before my fifteenth birthday, I met my first kindred spirit in a neighbouring town.

A mutual friend was having one of those teenage house parties that end up taking over the entire building and involve lots of loud music. I was there in my long tie-dyed skirt, fishnet top and yellow DMs – I'd hunted everywhere for them because I didn't want to wear the same colour shoes as everyone else – and that's when I spotted Paul in his white ruffled shirt and bondage pants. He'd recently bleached his long hair and had synthetic extensions added; I remember being surprised as I had assumed that all goths had black hair. We were the only two goths in the room and soon struck up a friendship.

Paul was about seventeen or eighteen and went to the local college so was instantly much cooler than any of the other boys I knew. During the week, after our classes, we'd meet up in the graveyard by the war memorial where we'd sit and discuss music. At 5.30pm sharp, we'd walk up to the train station to go our separate ways and at the weekends, he'd often meet me for lunch outside the high street clothing store where I worked on Saturdays. My parents were quite strict and I wasn't allowed to dye or shave my hair so I used to encourage Paul to carry out the hair experiments that I dreamed of. The week that Paul followed my instructions to create an electric blue Mohawk was when the area manager turned up. I can still see the look of horror and disgust on her face when a grinning Paul appeared at the door, with his massive hair, full-on goth make-up and a leather jacket with the band name "Alien Sex Fiend" painted on the back. I thought he looked brilliant but she disagreed and asked him to move further down the road so he wouldn't scare the customers!

Saturday nights meant one thing: Slimelight. I was too young to go but Paul went and every Monday, he'd tell me all about the goths, punks and bikers that he'd met on his adventures. The club is probably one of the world's most famous goth nights but it started off as a squat party and had only recently moved to its permanent home; a large concrete building known as Electrowerkz (it used to house a metal works). The entry policy at that time was really strict: you either had to be a member or get signed in by one and every member had to answer a tough questionnaire to prove they were a real goth. Back then, Slimelight didn't have a bar but there was a coffee shop where you could buy heavily-sweetened extra-strong coffee, so thick you could practically stand a spoon in it, and chocolate bars to give you enough energy to dance until the tube station reopened the following morning. As the venue was unlicensed at the time, people used to bring in their own alcoholic drinks and I recall talk of moonshine being shared between black-clad beings. I thought it sounded like the most amazing place and decided I would go as soon as I was old enough to. Eventually I did! It was just the way I'd imagined it and I even recognised some of the characters from Paul's colourful tales. Many, many years later, it's still a club I frequent.

I lost touch with Paul when I was about sixteen. As we walked up to the train station for the last time, he told me he'd quit college and was going back to live with his parents. I remember he was wearing this wonderful brocade jacket, PVC jeans and satin gloves with large, silver rings sparkling on his fingers. But when we walked onto the platform, I spotted a whole group of girls from my school – I hadn't realised that Take That were playing at Wembley Arena and half my year were on their way to see them. With their mothers. I was so embarrassed and one of the mums actually banned her daughter from socialising with me afterwards because she was horrified to see me walking around with a guy in make-up and, what she considered to be, outrageous clothing!

I was nineteen when I finally visited Slimelight myself. I searched for Paul through the haze of clove cigarette smoke, dry ice and incense but I never found him. In fact, it was another few years before I bumped into him at a completely different club by which time, he was a cybergoth and dressed head-to-toe in UV-reactive white clothing! The funniest thing is, I wasn't the only fledgling goth he influenced. I'm forever meeting people who tell me how he changed their lives. He's become quite iconic!

Natasha Scharf.

★ ★ ★

Simon, a fan of The Mission and Goth in general.

I know that for a lot of Goths, bands such as The Mission and Sisters of Mercy were very much at the more mainstream, 'rockier' end of the genre. Indeed, I am aware that some purist Goths are of the opinion that these sort of bands were not even goth at all, that in their view they were rather more just an evolution of rock bands. That's their opinion, of course, and there is certainly some evidence for them to support that.

However, subculture has one asset that is more apparent than any other – it is *subjective*. So, for me at least, growing up in Warwickshire in the 80s and 90s, goth for me was listening to those bands. I didn't dress the Full Goth Monty, I didn't wear make-up and pointy boots, and I didn't read gothic literature. But I did listen to bands like The Mission, Sisters, All About Eve and so on, pretty obsessively.

I met The Mission's lead singer, Wayne Hussey at a festival, once. He was wearing a cowboy hat, boots and a long flowing black coat/cloak. He looked amazing. He was also one of the nicest and most approachable blokes you could wish to meet. I always thought this band was the best of the gothic rock lot, a fact backed up by their festival appearances and international tours.

Like I said, I wasn't dressing as a goth myself. I was a 'secret' goth almost. It wasn't that I wasn't interested but I was pretty quiet and under-confident and where I lived there was quite a bit of 'goth bashing' at times, so I just was a bit fearful of going down that route. Maybe I should've just done it and said bollocks! I certainly never had the encyclopaedic knowledge of goth music and music in general that a lot of Goths do − I still think it is one of the most intelligent and considered of all the tribes. Goths might be quiet at times, but they bloody well know their music!

I always really liked the female goth look. The long, thick black hair, dark flowing clothes, exaggerated make-up, the tall boots, it was sexy and cool. The goth male could often dress very similarly, although I never found that quite so sexy, haha!

Goth is, along with perhaps skinhead and Mod, one of the most long-lasting of all the tribes. Maybe Goth never goes out of fashion because it was never in fashion. You still see Goths wandering around pretty much any city you go to, and it is true that there almost always seems to be 'the only goth in the village', even in rural Britain. That in itself is testament to the lasting power of Goth.

Simon.

MODS

*A contribution from Jenny,
a Scottish female Mod.*

In the summer of 1982 I was 12 and a half, lived in a crappy small town on the east of Scotland, I'd also just started secondary school and musically, up until that point, the records I was buying were either by Adam and the Ants or The Police. By 1982 the Mod Revival in my town was in full swing, but it was starting secondary school which exposed me to all the other music out there – I'd been listening to '60s stuff for years, thanks to my Dad having fairly good taste in music – but it was all clicking together, The Who, The Animals, The Yardbirds, Rolling Stones all playing a medley in my head, and then I heard The Jam. I must've been aware of them over the years, in fact, I remember religiously taping the Top 40 every Sunday and 'Going Underground' being number 1, that was probably the song that 'Jennifer, your tea's ready' is recorded over, with 'but I'm taping the charts, Mum' making an appearance too. So, 'Just Who Is The 5 O'Clock Hero?', 'The Bitterest Pill' and 'Beat Surrender' and then that was that. Bugger, whilst I was listening to The Police and *Ghost in the Machine*, I should've been listening to The Gift, arse!

So it was a bleak start to 1983, but all was not lost. I managed to pick up a few after school jobs, a paper round, a Friday evening milk round and weekend waitressing, so I had cash. On Saturday afternoons I headed to Dundee for the record exchange shop Groucho's. Oh, what a shop, hundreds upon thousands of records, and a couple of very helpfully categorised boxes labelled "mod and soul". This continued for a number of years, every Saturday you'd find me rummaging in the boxes buying up the back catalogue of The Jam and The Specials and bits and pieces by '60s bands I'd heard of – I hate to think about all the tunes I overlooked, because I'd not heard of them. There were fanzines too, Groucho's stocked 007, I was buying clothes from Cavern, not very good quality, but I thought I was fab.

It was difficult being a Mod aged 13; none of the girls in my year were really into it, the musical interests of the group I went about with ranged from Duran Duran (blah), Shakin' Stevens? And Simple Minds, so not really any chance of us learning from each other. I expect throughout the first year I was still discovering the sounds which would stay with me, and then one year on from starting secondary school, The Style Council came on the scene. I'd been reading about Paul Weller's new group in the likes of *Smash Hits*, but for some reason I took an extreme dislike to Tracey Young. I'm sure she's a lovely girl, but I'd read an interview with her which really irked me, and out of principal (or bloody mindedness) I refused to entertain the mere suggestion of listening to, never mind actually enjoying 'Speak Like A Child'. It was my dad, once more, I can thank. He reckoned I'd really like them if only I'd give the song a chance. So I did, and that was that, a life-changing moment, sounds dramatic, and it probably is. I loved the song, loved the look, I was a Mod. The band opened my eyes and ears to something new and magical. And as the Style Council years continued, I'd buy everything I could which featured the band, taped every programme they were on, I still have a few VHS videos worth of performances ranging from Wigan to *Saturday Superstore* to cooler TV programmes like *The Tube*.

The Mods were all the older guys 2 or 3 years above me at High School, who were so cool riding up and down the High Street on their scooters, but it wasn't the done thing to hang out with them. It was kind of crap really, when I hear folk talking now about how fantastic it was being a teenage Mod... back then, the camaraderie, the friendships which have gone on to last a lifetime, it wasn't like that for me. In fact, it was quite isolating, me in my dog tooth ski pants, polo neck jumpers, little dresses and pointy shoes, but I persevered, kept buying records – I was still following the Style Council and listening intently to the words of Paul Weller, getting into Red Wedge and the Faith Brothers, but I had also started listening to Soul, more specifically the sounds of Curtis Mayfield and Otis Redding, although for some reason it was '70s Mayfield I was digging, The Impressions would come along later. I remember one of my favourite albums at the time was Otis Blue and kicking around somewhere in my house is a very badly recorded cassette of The Action's *The Ultimate! Action* which I played to death. I was reading what I could about the '60s, quizzing my folks about what to wear, and then like a miracle from above, *Ready Steady Go* was repeated on Channel 4. It was shown on a Friday evening, 5.30pm rings bells, and so I'd head out on my milk round at 5, do half the round, come home for tea and watch *RSG*. It was fantastic; it gave a focus to everything I was doing. Now I could actually see what the girls were wearing, what they were doing with their hair and the music that was being played. That would've been about 1985 and I continued to have my own wee scene in my bedroom, probably went to some parties, and remember going to a Mod ball in Dundee in 1986 once I'd turned 16 and was "apparently" a bit more responsible. The music being played then was very much the Wigan Casino *Classics Compilation* album, you know... 'The Snake', 'No1 In My

Heart', 'Ski-ing in the Snow', to be honest, it didn't fill me with inspiration.

In the summer of 1986, four years on from my epiphany, I moved to the arse end of nowhere, for four months to work, when I returned home, the mods had disappeared. Everyone was either a Scooterist or a Casual and then finally mere months before my 18th birthday when I could actually go out and drink, the tunes had changed and the clubs would play a solitary half hour of Northern Soul – Nine Times out of ten anyone???

Through my late teens and early 20s I was listening to other tunes and sounds, saw The James Taylor Quartet in about 1989 at Fat Sam's in Dundee, they were fab but nobody seemed to dig them, there was no Style Council then, and I probably became a bit more influenced by the sounds of my then-boyfriend. He was into grunge, which wasn't my thing, I was dabbling with a more '50s look, baseball jackets, quiff, turned up jeans with DM boots, I thought I looked great. Didn't really do the Acid Jazz thing, I bought a Galliano album because I read somewhere that Mick Talbot was involved with the band. The relationship with Grunge boy fizzled out, but my first love... Paul Weller came back into my life with his debut solo album, and finally, in 1993 I saw him live at the Barrowlands in Glasgow, YES!!!!! I'd never got a chance to see the Style Council, a combination of overprotective parents, and well... overprotective parents meant I couldn't go to Glasgow or Edinburgh and when a gig in Dundee was finally announced, I quickly bought my ticket, and then it was cancelled. Nae luck!!!

I wasn't doing the all-nighters and rallies like so many of my now peers were doing, I didn't know anybody who had been or still was a mod so, like the '80s, the '90s were spent following Paul Weller, buying lots of Kent releases and getting on with life, work and kids.

The new century was a new beginning for me. We got internet access and I started contributing to some Mod forums, the early days of Modculture.com, Mod Revival and the first Paul Weller forum. I made friends, who are still friends now, there would be meet ups with the Paul Weller forums, I heard about club nights and gigs happening around Scotland, my now ex-husband and I went to see The Jamm (Jam tribute band) on numerous occasions in Glasgow, met up with folks at Paul Weller gigs. I was astounded to discover that there was still a Mod Scene, it hadn't disappeared, only gone a little quiet. I had two young kids at this point, so couldn't do as much as I'd have liked, but with the internet, I could keep up with what was going on.

There must be something about the summertime because in August 2003, I went to Goodfoot in Glasgow with my friend Jacqui – who I'd met on one of the Weller forums. Goodfoot was a long running soul night, I was nervous, this was the first scene night I'd attended in nearly 20 years, what if I'd lost my dance moves, was I dressed right? Bloody hell, people were up dancing ON THEIR OWN!!!!! I was so out of touch, there were Skins at a Soul do – my last experience of Skinheads was the Oi crowd of the early '80s, this was mad, but I loved it, the music was wonderful and I wanted to do this all the time.

Then I met Colin. He was a friend of Jacqui's, a Mod and was involved with Glasgow's Mod Club Friday Street. Colin is now my husband, and when circumstances allowed, we went to different clubs in Scotland, down to London for Crossfire, Leeds, Manchester and Rimini. I was hearing different sounds, bye bye Northern Soul, hello R&B; I got back into collecting records, and on occasion djing too. I organised a few nights and then started helping with Friday Streets PR and promotions. I helped book Andy Lewis for a Paul Weller after-show party, through this involvement I met Andy Crofts, Steve Craddock and – it's only taken 25 years – Paul Weller.

A couple of years ago I started a mod fanzine with my friend Sharon Wood – *Double Breasted* Modzine is doing great and has been responsible for so many positive experiences. I've met many wonderful people through the fanzine, subscribers, advertisers and contributors, 'legends' like John Hellier, 'Mumper' Bax, Smiler, Dave Edwards, Guy Joseph and Eddie Pillar. My record reviews have put me in touch with Rich at Acid Jazz, Alex at Copasetic, I'm speaking to people all over the world, Mexico, Brazil, Hong Kong, hearing new music, interviewing bands and organising more gigs. Last year I put together a CD compilation of current Scottish Mod/60s influenced bands (*A Little Mixed Up*), this turned into an all-dayer with 7 of the bands and I now have a record label which has released an album from The Laynes. I'm managing a band, and in 2010 *A Little Mixed Up 2* brought DC Fontana and The Universal to Scotland. Early in 2010, a chance meeting with Gary and Simon from the Purple Hearts at a book launch developed into me promoting both the Purple Hearts and The Chords gigs in Glasgow, the first time either band had played in Scotland for over 25 years. It's been amazing to see so many happy faces watching bands they worshipped as young mods back in the early '80s.

I remember having a conversation with a 'grunge' friend about 15 years ago when I was 25. A guy drove past on a Vespa, and I turned to my pal and said, "When I was a mod, I always wanted a Vespa." His response, "Jen; you'll always be a Mod." This conversation makes me think of what's being said nowadays about the so-called "Mod Life Crisis." You never stop being a Mod, you might not be going to clubs, or being 'Seen on the Scene', but just because you didn't regularly attend Club (insert name) in 1995 or a Rally in 2000 because you had a young family, doesn't make you any less of a Mod than the guy who did.

I'm 40, have 4 kids and am having the time of my life.

*Jenny Baillie (*Double Breasted *fanzine).*

★ ★ ★

Dickie's account of scooters, mates and trying to pull.

We didn't really have a plan Lee and I, all we knew that there was a scooter rally in Weymouth at the weekend and we were going. I had only ever known the local scooter ride outs and the mod rallies to Margate before and were hearing the stories of the big scooter club weekends around the country and thought this is where all the mods go, not just hop on the train to London and hang out in Carnaby Street or Kensington indoor market then wait until somewhere like the Groovy cellar opened and stood at the back looking at all the much cooler than ours clothes they were wearing. We wanted something bigger, a couple of hundred scooters in a car park in Margate was nothing, and we wanted to see thousands.

We didn't have much money between us, so decided to save costs and go to Weymouth on just the one scooter, mine. So that Wednesday morning we spent cleaning the scooter and bolting a few more lights and mirrors on and made a sign for the back, The Arrivals scooter club, 1983 Margate to Weymouth Trans Global Express. There wasn't a scooter club as such, just Lee and I, we were sort of between clubs, the Triple S scooter club had recently sort of dwindled away (still have my patch though, and that of the Kent Coasters before that) so we started one ourselves that morning, and we thought it sounded cool, a bit like a name that could be used for a mod band, and the Trans Global part was from The Jam track.

The following conversation took place, but I can't remember now who said which line.

"So what shall we do now?"

"Let's just go."

"But it's Wednesday."

"Yeh, let's just take our time and see who we can pick up on the way, we can go up through the Medway towns then across to Maidstone and across country, bound to be lots of mods going and we can crash out wherever".

So off we went, tent and pack on the back and modded up. Late afternoon on a Wednesday isn't really a hive of mod activity in Chatham town centre (we had always thought of Chatham as a mod mecca around that time, so many people from there used to come down to Margate at the weekends). The scooter was parked up behind the shopping centre and we just wondered about from café to café looking for the local mod hang out, there must be one we thought, every little town had one and this was a big town, must be one, then we met Tracy. Don't know who saw who first or where exactly, but this lovely girl in green trench coat and ski-pants and short blond French crop asked if we were in town for the gig tomorrow night, going to be lots of mods there.

"Yeh, of course," we replied together, our chance to meet up with loads of others for a big ride down to Weymouth we thought.

"Just need somewhere to stay tonight."

"You can stay at mine."

We couldn't believe our luck.

"Wow, is that your scooter, will you take me for a ride in the morning?"

"Of course," I said, Lee was not amused and gave me a scowl.

So the next morning we told Lee we wouldn't be long, just nipping over to Maidstone so Tracy could pick up some new shoes for the do that night.

He wasn't amused when we got back six hours later, he'd been dressed up ready for the do for hours, but we had just got on well and were enjoying each other's company, oh well he'd get over it, he didn't.

There were a lot of mods at The King Charles Hotel in Gillingham (a venue that was used so many times over the years, and I have great memories of so many bands there, best of all though was the one-off Christmas show that The Prisoners did there when they reformed for a couple of gigs in the mid-90s, was very privileged to have been there for that) that night and we had a great night of dancing and drinking, not so much Lee though, but oh well I'd met a lovely girl, I know selfish, but hey ho! I'm sure it was Geno Washington that night, but can't say I took much notice of the band, was too busy chatting with Tracy and having fun.

Only problem was, we hadn't met anyone that was going to Weymouth. So Friday morning it was kiss Tracy goodbye and a somewhat annoyed Lee climbed aboard and we were off on our way to Weymouth, be there in a few hours we thought, how wrong we were.

Somewhere near the Kent border we were travelling down the main street of Westerham (I think it was called) a narrow street lined with shops and a narrow pavement, with a bend in the road, I took the bend only to find a zebra crossing and on that crossing a little old lady being helped across by a police woman, up and over she went, leaving a trail of Brussel sprouts from her shopping. I parked the scooter up, looked back at Lee who was just sat there with a shocked look on his face, looked over at the gathering crowd round the old lady checked to see if I could do anything, then re-adjusted my mirrors back to where they were, Lee was still sitting there, a shopkeeper came out, "You all right son, want a cup of tea? Don't worry, it will be all right, been trying to get that crossing moved for years, so dangerous…" The thought of the poor old lady on the floor upset me for quite a while after.

We spent the rest of the afternoon at the local police station, and was quite late by the time they let us be on our way, they did me for a faulty brake light bulb and a few months later three points on my license for driving without due care, but I wasn't fined because of the mitigating circumstances that the crossing had been put in a dangerous place, the poor old lady and her shopping all over the place is still etched in my mind.

It was way after midnight as we saw the signs for Weymouth 5 miles, there were a few scooters parked up in a layby and a stall set up selling scrumpy in five litre plastic containers, the sort you bulk buy washing up liquid in for restaurants and hotels, but it was bloody cheap and as we couldn't afford much else a couple of these were bungeed on to the scooter. The drive into town was uneventful and we followed the signs for the so-called campsite, this was a tarmac car park next to a go-kart track, people had tried to pitch tents as best they could, we were walking through the dark, were very down and looking for the best place when we heard "Dickie, over here, mate." It was Jay, one of the Herne Bay crowd, "There's a patch of grass next to our tent, it's on a bit of a slope though, but it will do."

After our feeble attempts at putting up a tent on 45 degree slope we sat with Jay and others listening to music and scooter engines, downing Scrumpy (with a rather strange after taste, never buy from lay-by sellers). It wasn't long before we found that we were in the minority on this rally, the minority being mods! It seemed that every other type of person rode a scooter here, this was new and strange to us young mods, Skinheads, Punks, people in denim and leather, looking like the rockers that chased us and we chased back in Margate, but on scooters, but scooters the like of which we had never seen, little or no panels, extended forks, matt black or camouflaged, we didn't realise at the time how much this would affect us. The rest of the weekend went by pretty uneventful and we left for home on the Bank Holiday Monday morning with about three pounds between us, which meant we ran out of fuel in Brighton and had to syphon petrol from somewhere, this done we made it home coasting the last few miles on fumes. I only ever saw Lee once again after that weekend, don't blame him really, I wasn't much of a mate abandoning him for the day and then putting him in shock, guess he'd had enough.

As for me the scooterist had arrived on the scene, and gradually over the next few months the mod scene had pretty much died out around us, a far cry from the days when we were bolting as many accessories as we could on our scooters, people were cutting down their scooter panels and out came the matt green paint, and scooterists we became, although I kept my scooters pretty much whole, I still preferred that look and instead of customizing with accessories I found I loved custom paintwork and engraving, but the scooterist rallies were not for too long for me although I went to quite a few and had a lot of fun with some great mates, something in me missed the mod scene and the smarter clothes and to my mind the better music. By 86/7 I had started going to the CCI mod rallies, first of all in nearby Hastings this is where my heart was and then came The Untouchables weekenders, much better still, I had found my place. Another couple of years and it was then The New Untouchables [Nut's], perfection for me, the music scene had shifted for me from soul-based to the music of 66 and beyond and my love of all Mod/60s style of music was growing more and more and I couldn't get enough, it was like 'feed me more tunes', I tried to make it to every Nut's event I could, regularly leaving work on a Saturday afternoon, driving to the Purple Pussycat or The Electric something or rather, Mousetrap etc., partying all night, crashing out for an hour or two then driving back to be at work on a Sunday morning. The mod scene was designed for people that worked weekends.

I became a regular at the clubs in London, so much so that I soon found myself talked into working for them by my old mate Rob, even let me do a bit of Dj'ing a couple of times, and that was that for the next god knows how long, travelling to every all-nighter, weekender, here, in Europe (where I met the lovely young lady that became my wife on a mod party on a Rhine boat cruise) and even to the States, with a wonderful bunch of mad eccentric crazy lovable friends, seeing the most amazing bands, too many to list here, but bands of young and some not so young people playing covers and their own material, with fantastic tunes and now highly sought after records, or trying their best to sound like their heroes from the '60s, and seeing some of those very heroes live (or in some case almost live), and for me meeting many of them at sound checks or before and after shows, that was my life, the Nut's, and I bloody loved every minute of it (well nearly).

Dickie (Nut's retired... mostly).

★ ★ ★

Adam from Rowed Out Records – 'FOR A SUSSED GENERATION'.

I don't think my introduction to Mod is any different to anyone else of my generation. I was born in 1972, thus missing the original revival of 1979, only latching on in around 83 as an eleven year old at school. The 'big lads' at the time had moved on from Mods to scooter boys and that meant they didn't want their suits, button down shirts and most importantly, their records anymore. It only took one enterprising younger brother to bring his siblings clothes to school along with a few cassettes of The Kinks and the first Who LP and that was it – I was hooked. I remember buying an old Ben Sherman and I think a few cassettes with my pocket money... but that wasn't enough. Around that time after The Jam had split, Paul Weller was in The Style Council, a more poppy band and that meant I could read about them in *Smash Hits* and *Record Mirror* and I could also see what Weller was wearing then (remember this was 83/84 when Weller was at his smartest). This led me to backtrack and buy the customary Parka and hunt around Millets for a boating blazer. I was quite happy progressing to being the only Mod in the school (what had started as about 10-15 dwindled down to me). I was also the only mod within a 10-mile radius of where I lived (a small town in Buckinghamshire). I began to research more as I hit 14/15 years old and Mum and Dad often went to London sightseeing, which meant I could have a wander down Carnaby Street and the first time I wandered into The Cavern, it literally blew me away. Racks and racks of suits just like I had seen in pictures, jumpers, button downs, Sta-Prest and scarfs. A walk upstairs and a poky little room had all the latest releases on vinyl, along with badges, posters and videos. A few yards down from Ganton Street was The Merc which had even more vinyl etc. Over the next year or so I must have spent all my paper round and first job wages on LPs and singles by The Times, Makin' Time, The Kick, The Moment, The Scene etc. along with those lovely Kent compilations.

The next logical step was a scooter. My under-15 football manager, Colin, had been a revival mod and still had a couple of scooters in a garage. Now remember again this is around 1987, so I gladly parted with around £100 for a Vespa 50 Special and a Vespa 90, both of which were pushed home and the restoration began. The 50 Special had 'Nine below Zero' on the side, which was then covered in white spray and a hastily-made template of the first Specials LP was made and sprayed on in black. Tassels for the handlebars, fly screen, back rack and chrome wheel covers, and of course crash bars laden with mirrors were purchased. My perfect mod scooter!

It was late 87 that I caught my first glimpse of Mods en masse. The Great Yarmouth CCI rally was taking place where I was on holiday at the time and the sights were amazing, hundreds of scooters, well dressed kids and for me as a 15 year old it was my idea of heaven. Luckily I had packed my Cavern Dogtooth suit and my dad kindly took me to Gorleston-On-Sea for my first taste of a Mod do. The James Taylor Quartet was the live band. I had no idea at the time of any of the songs being spun by the DJs but knew I had to be a part of this. I met a chap from Luton during the day and we kept in touch during 1988 and by 1989 I was ready to travel to my first rally on a scooter. How the hell I managed to get from near Aylesbury all the way to Lowestoft without a spare tyre, AA cover or even the basic tools I still don't know, but when I arrived on the Friday to be greeted by hundreds of like-minded people it didn't matter that I couldn't feel my backside or my thumbs. That year I managed I think six or seven rallies (we used to haggle over spending more than £10 on a night's B&B, £7 or £8 was the norm!). I was also now in The Moreton Parkas A.M.S. (you had to be affiliated back then) and the group of us spent 1990 the same as we had the year before travelling all over the UK without a care on 125 scooters. The bands I saw were also amazing; The Clique, The Babysnakes, The Boys (pre-Ocean Colour Scene), The Moment, Small World.

I was also a tailored Mod by now; hours were spent in 'Textile King' on Wardour Street looking at material, then once the correct mohair was sifted, it was the five minute walk to 'Charlie' to get measured up. Really nice guy, always pleasant, with his wife in the corner beavering away on the sewing machine. Charlie used to give a discount to the Mods and his tiny office was always packed on Saturdays – standing room only! I must have had a dozen suits made; I had jeans and cords made too. Katy Stevens was the shirt maker to go to as well, again a nice lady who always had ideas for shirts – contrasts, extra buttons etc – real attention to detail.

The Mod scene in 1990/91 was different then from five years previous, it had become more elitist, smarter and basically tightened up. The CCI rallies had become a bit passé, Dee-Lite and The Charlatans were being played and that put a lot of people off. The Untouchables started their own rallies along with The Rhythm & Soul Set. I attended all three variants during 90 and 91; to me, The Rhythm & Soul Set rallies were the best, loads of quality jazz and R&B, club soul and British beat, just what I wanted to hear. The rallies then were great times I was 18/19 and loving it! Tailored, scooter, growing record collection, nearly perfected Marriott hair, good group of friends and a proper Mod. Work and the week got in the way, I just wanted to get out and dance and be part of a scene. Friday night was spent in either

Euston station for the club there, or maybe Circles. Saturday was The Mildmay Tavern and then, later, Drummonds on Euston Road and Sunday was the best, The Kings Tavern in Reading. The closest I think anyone could have got to replicating The Scene (as we hoped it would have been) or Tiles. The music was blinding, just R&B, both British and American, hardly ever any Northern Soul, just Motown now and again, the odd ska record and then loads of jazz. Tracks like 'Crawdaddy Simone', 'Bring it to Jerome', 'Think twice before you go', 'Walkin', even Van Morrison's 'Moon dance'. Everyone was suited, both boys and girls, and it didn't matter it finished at eleven as it was a relief after the whole weekend spent scooting everywhere!

I attended the rallies and various clubs regularly all over the country (including the infamous 'Blankenberge') up until the late '90s, but it went a bit too psychedelic for me and also most others, but my interest didn't dwindle – I still collected records, got more scooters, dressed the same. My interest was rekindled in the early 2000s by clubs like 'Shotgun' and the 'Mousetrap' R&B all-nighters; I also started to attend more Northern Soul clubs around the Peterborough area as I had moved up that way. Lincolnshire may be a horrible place to live but they like their soul up there which proved an okay contrast.

Around the mid-2000s there was also a growing interest in late '50s/early '60s RnB or 'popcorn', a scene started in Belgium in the '70s. New DJs were emerging and bringing with them their influences from other genres. Personally I'm not a fan of this style of music, Mod RnB to me will always be Sonny Boy Williamson, John Lee Hooker and Slim Harpo et al, but I can recognise a need for progression and if it makes the scene attract newer, younger faces who will bring with them a regenerative attitude then so be it. The scene had turned into an almost 'Saga' night with most attendees in their late 30s/early 40s or older – the same as I had noticed on the Northern Soul circuit – moving forward to 2010 and the mod scene in the UK is back on its feet thanks to a handful of young, enthusiastic Mods prepared to put on nights/clubs. Good luck to them, may they carry the torch onwards, it was after all, supposed to be a 'youth cult'!

In 2006 I decided to start my own record label as I had always been jealous of Dizzy's success at Detour Records and thought I would have a stab at that! I approached the first band The Shake (now The Screenbeats) and pressed up 300 7" singles, this was followed by a CD compilation and another couple of EPs. In 2009 I really went for it – not for any ego reasons (I find it hard to do sales face to face), just because there are some great bands out there. I loved The Shake; The Patterns from Manchester are just like The Prisoners; The Lost 45s from Leeds also. The scene musically is now very healthy, but without it being strictly mod in the sense of the word I grew up with. The sound is the same, but the dress sense is different – no '60s or suits, still smart though.

It's now 2010, I've still got my scooter (as has Abby, my wife), still got the records, still collecting 45s (as, again, is my wife), still getting clothes tailor-made – now at George Lilley in Leeds, rather than Charlie and still very much into a scene that has seen me go from young lad to father of two (my old clothes are still under my bed in the vain hope that either Sam or Ben will want to follow my path! I can hope!!!!).

So on reflection, Mod has been to me, a way of life, clichéd, but ultimately true, it occupied my teens, twenties and now thirties. I still dress the same, always smart, always mod or my interpretation of it, still crave that GS 160, still have a big wants list for 45s and still look down on other fashions as inferior. That has been my life as a mod, I was lucky to be around, as a teenager, a big mod scene and those memories will stay with me forever, wherever Mod may go in the future I will follow as I believe it to be the only cult worth following, always evolving, always exciting.

Adam.

★ ★ ★

'The Style Counselled' by Steve White.

I was at a certain age when there was much more of a clear-cut edge regards to youth factions. And by the age of being thirteen or fourteen the need to belong to a tribe was very apparent which unfortunately now kids just want to be like everybody else. So back then being thirteen or fourteen it was like someone would go away on holiday and when they came back they kind of had an ear pierced and had a safety pin and it was like over the course of the holiday they had discovered punk.

The mod thing was fairly big around south London which was where I used to hang around with friends, so places like Bermondsey and the Old Kent Road. There was a big fascination with The Jam and the similar bands of the time but it was mainly The Jam at the time which I never really got. For some reason I remember kind of toying with the idea of getting a tonic jacket but it just never felt really me. At that point I was discovering black music and I was really into discovering funk and soul.

By this time I had already been playing drums since I was eight. I was into bands like Kool and the Gang, Earth Wind and Fire and funky jazz. And there were still deejays like Chris Hill and Robbie Vincent that were playing that. And there were pubs down the Old Kent Road that had nights playing this stuff so I used to go down and just listen from outside these pubs. With these places there was a definite style thing. People wore bright coloured polo shirts and stone wash jeans and I just wanted to look like those guys.

Then when I was older enough to get into these places I went to a disco held in a pub called The Falcon in Eltham. There was a very mixed crowd of black kids and white kids and they were what we called Soul Boys. We didn't call them Casuals, we called them Soul Boys. So on the nights that I used to get in I would stand there and listen to the music and watch these black guys dance. They would dance fantastic and wear vests, peg trousers (that people used to get from Lewisham market) and Jam shoes.

I recently saw a clip of The Style Council on *Top of the Pops*. We were doing 'Long Hot Summer' for the Christmas special in 1983 and I was wearing a red Lyle and Scot cardigan, Lois jeans and a Ben Sherman re-issue shirt that Millets did at that time, a pair of Nike trainers and it was funny because I had a whistle hanging around my neck. Now that whistle was just part of the uniform that we used to wear around that time when we went to the clubs. It was all part of that soul patrol sort of thing. So watching these boys at these soul pubs and clubs was where my influences came from.

In London we had a very different kind of thing to what was going on in the north. In the north it was all about the football and purely about the terraces but in London it was much more integrated with the music. There were hooligan gangs like the Headhunters and the I.C.F but it wasn't based around fashion in the same way it was up north. I remember first seeing the look at places like Tranmere because that was where I went, being a Charlton supporter.

So I used to see these Tranmere supporters coming down, not so much in Lacoste but they did wear tracky tops. So they would have a cheap tee shirt or jumper but there would be one thing that they would be wearing that was nice and that they had saved up for. We were the same. We would save up for one nice item, say a pair of trainers but when you got home you would kind of put them back in the box after giving them a little clean and tidy up. I mean nowadays you can go to JD Sports and buy a whole collection of Adidas classics but back then buying just one thing was something that we aspired to.

So for me, having this cross over between being into Soul music and going to football then suddenly I was being in this band. The next thing I know I was playing in Italy, France and Amsterdam and I was actual able to go and buy this stuff. I mean

I was now earning. The first time I ever went to Paris I went to buy a Lacoste for real. Up until then I had been wearing Cecil Gee polos that were their version of the Lacoste style. So with my first bit of money from The Style Council I went out and bought ten of them in ten different colours.

Then we really started touring I remember going to Italy and we were getting their Ultras coming along (they were never really welcome but they were there). But they used to wear the faded Lacoste, skinny jeans and desert boots. So then being seventeen and suddenly being able to afford it I used to spend all my money on clothes. It was either drums or clothes.

In London there were a few places that you buy the stuff from. There was a shop (Nik Naks) on the corner of Wardour Street that was really, really expensive and I bought the jumper that I wore in the 'Shout to the Top' video which was a red Kappa jumper that I paid £240 in 1983 which was a bloody fortune at the time. But I just wanted this jumper. In my eyes it was the most beautiful thing and it was like the jumper that Art Blakey wore in 1956.

At this time it was the Italian labels like the Kappa and Tacchinis that people wanted but it was still incredibly limited as to what people could get. The styles and colours were limited but once I started to get abroad I just found it very interesting to start discovering these new brands. When I started buying Lacoste it was from a shop called the Mad Hatter in Amsterdam. It's still there near the American Hotel. I went there with my son when it was his eighteenth and bought him a Lacoste. That shop was where them black and orange scarves that we wore in The Style Council came from.

Other places around London were Moda 3 in Bermondsey (before re-locating to Blackheath). Mickey Moda made the leather jackets that Paul (Weller) used to wear during that time when he launched his solo career. Mickey could have made loads of money but he was a bit of visionary and I think he had a lot of his stuff ripped off by bigger designers. In the 'Sunflower' video that jacket Paul wears is a Moda jacket.

Another place was Dickie Dirts which was an old converted cinema. We used to go and get our Levi's jeans from there. Cecil Gee was another place, Woodhouse another. Then where we used to record near Marble Arch was a Pringle shop. I used to get paid on a Thursday and go straight to the shop to treat myself. I remember a mint green and white pullover. The thing was that Paul was the one who was very recognisable but a lot of that kind of clobber was what I was actually wearing at the time. But as soon as Paul started wearing it then that was it, so did loads of others. And it's true that Paul Weller also went out and bought ten or so Pringle jumpers from that shop one day. I had just come back to the studio with this green and cream jumper with blue rings around the arms. It was a real fancy design. It was about thirty eight quid. So I went back into the studio with this jumper and Paul then went out and came back with a big bag of them.

When I joined the Style Council that was what I used to wear and Paul had been into the Paris thing. If we went to do a TV show I just wore what I normally wore. I didn't take a change of clothes. I remember one of the first parties that I ever went to with The Style Council in a place called Bananas just off Oxford Street. I remember I was wearing Adidas shell toes and faded Lois jeans and that was my look and what all the kids were wearing.

Mick (Talbot) was never really into the look. He liked Lacoste and he always liked to wear a nice pair of shoes like some brogues or penny loafers. But Lacoste was his thing and still to this day he likes a nice Lacoste. And that all had to do with our French connection. And I still love a Lacoste. I mean they last. I have got Lacoste that are ten years old.

I remember Dean Powell the boxing trainer telling me that he wanted to get some Adidas Sambas because he had seen me wearing some red ones. Back then if you weren't a mod, you weren't a goth, you weren't a punk then you was a Soul Boy.

"Bikers – an ongoing and inspirational Way of Life that has
become an intrinsic part of our daily DNA."

Britpop mined many areas of British culture, including music,
fashion, live shows and literature.

Casuals were obsessively particular about the right labels and look. This is the band Accent.

"For a period (all too brief sadly), grebo mattered and that fact can never be denied."

Natascha Scharf (left), goth expert and author; (right) Goth is one of the longest and most multi-layered of all subcultures.

Scooters adorned with mirrors and ready for the next rally.

Both skinhead and Mod are two of the most meticulous and exacting
of all the Tribes in terms of fashion and style.

Will Hunt Vincent and Claire Russell. As Will says, "I'm pleased and proud to have played my part in what has to be the coolest underground music scene in existence. Long may it continue."

The legendary Wigan Casino, the epicentre of Northern Soul.

Little Jo (left), founder of the seminal Alcoholic Rats website.

In reality, for most kids outside London, punk was not about the 'postcard punks' photographed in Trafalgar Square, but a less exaggerated look, as seen here.

Rave culture was marginalised by mainstream society at the time, but has recently begun to be recognised as one of the most influential youth cultures.

The Tribes have at times clashed violently and frequently. In the social media age, however, there is an overwhelming spirit of much greater mutual tolerance.

"Scooter boy encompassed all fashions from skinhead to psychobilly all drawn together with a passion for everything Lambretta and Vespa."

First generation skinhead, Nigel Harris (top and bottom right).
Legendary photographer, Gavin Watson, author of *Skins* (left).

Two Tone was a Tribe based on very particular fashions, an obsession with ska and related music genres and a fierce desire for racial equality.

But we never called ourselves Casuals, we were just Soul Boys.

Our Soul Boy look was much more related to music. I remember there was a time when Marks and Spencer's sold these wool crew neck jumpers and they looked nice with a pair of jeans, they weren't too expensive and it showed that it wasn't all about designer designer. It was more like, 'Yeah, that works'. Most people didn't have shit loads of money. I was lucky because I was in a very successful band and travelling to Italy and Japan. I still shopped locally and remember buying a deerstalker from Dunn and Co. I've still got one now. I wear it with my CP Company goggle coat.

The back cover to *Café Bleu* has me in a black and white shot-open stick position but I was actually wearing a tangerine crew neck. The thing is I'm not one to look back-play back on stuff that I've done but my partner Sally is a huge Style Council fan and always has been. 'Paris Match' is her favourite song of all time and she often says 'Look you've have really got to listen to this stuff again'. You know you put on *Café Bleu* and you have to remember that Paul Weller at that point was only twenty four years old. He just almost upset an entire nation of kids when they'd just split their favourite band up and he doesn't even sing until the fifth track. It's really is a brilliant record.

By the fact that I had never really connected with the mod scene when I first got to meet Paul I wasn't intimidated by him. I didn't try to be Rick Buckler so when Paul was playing tunes to me I wasn't thinking how would Rick do it. I was just playing bossa-novas. At the time Paul had a clear idea what he wanted to do. He wanted to try some orchestral stuff. I really just fell into it and it was a pleasure. The whole album came together in a very short space of time and it was very creative. I did my first gig with Paul on 25th May, 1983. I turned eighteen years old the following week.

When people talk pushing the boundaries and being experimental I think that was Paul's most experimental album.

The other day I was listening to *Café Bleu* because it came up on the iPod and his guitar playing is brilliant on that. He does some absolutely stunning phrasing on it. The whole album was done in a spirit of 'let's try and do something a bit different'. I think *Our Favourite Shop* is also a great record – just in a different way. *Café Bleu* was brave to do.

Being in The Style Council at that point was great. It was fantastic. I was eighteen years of age. The first flight I ever took was to Japan, I was thinking, *Shit, how smart is this?* and that was when the quest for the white Levi's began.

I remember Paul had said something about some reference to Steve McQueen wearing white Levi's in the '60s. I remember Paul buying some and there was something about the number of the jean. So in Japan there was these very kind of light-weight denim-almost chino and they were the rarest of the rare and in white, with the button fly, so we bought up almost every pair.

Those white Levi's had that similar look to what was on the *My Generation* album cover. There was that Levi's style jacket. I bought one similar to that in Japan. It would be worth a fortune now. So that was around 84–85 and that was how our obsession with white Levi's began.

By the late '80s I was into Italian jeans. I liked Diesel. I was still wearing Lacoste. I was still wearing Adidas trainers (I don't wear any other kind of trainer). It was around this time that I started to get into Stone Island. I would wear with a plain tee-shirt with a Stone Island jacket. This is a look I still adopt.

That was a busy period for me. I was doing stuff with Working Week, The James Taylor Quartet, Galliano and bits and pieces with the Jazz Renegades. So it was kind of a time when fashion was not the biggest pre-occupation for me. For myself it was just work and more work. I had also re-discovered a desire to practice so I was getting lots of drum lessons with Bob Armstrong (whom I'm still studying with). It was all very functional for me and wearing a good jacket was part of that.

My favourite jackets are CP Company. My pride and joy for a while was a leather goggle coat. But I put it on last year and thought, *Hmm, I'm too old for this now*, and so my son Curtis took it off me. I still have a blue parachute silk goggle coat. It's about five years old. I did a photo shoot in Japan and wore a Stone Island jacket. Stone Island saw the shoot and liked it and they gave me some stuff, a really nice black goggle coat. So now I have about four goggle coats. I've also got a green silk parachute combat style Stone Island jacket that I actually really love. I just love their summer stuff too. So that look of a nice jacket, tee-shirt pair of jeans and trainers or Sperry deck shoes is what I like.

I still like my clothes and still buy a lot of stuff. There's a shop that I like in Stockport called Infinities which is an old school casual shop. They are quite specific with what they sell. There's a guy called Danny that runs it with some other really young guys and they all look really cool and are all really into their clothes.

They do a nice bit of Ralph Lauren and Paul Smith. I like a bit of Paul Smith. The label has kind of got it right again. I have a Paul Smith jacket that is twenty five years old that I still wear. I like my Ralph Lauren in the summer with a pair of madras shorts and deck shoes.

Throughout the '90s I just continued being into the same stuff. I've never been pushed into wearing anything different. I do like a John Smedley though and if I could open a Smedley every morning, put it on and throw it away at the end of the day rather than having to dry-clean it, I'd be happy.

I still get the buzz of going shopping. I cannot go through an airport in Spain without buying a Lacoste and now I'm buying for my two year olds. I went to see The Stone Roses recently in a field. I don't like seeing bands in fields. It's not my style and was grizzling a bit so I went into this shop in Stockport and bought a Barbour with a limited edition Union Jack lining.

The thing is that when I first got that buzz for buying clothes, the stuff I was after was really hard to get. If you saw something you liked then often you had to save up to get it. Now everything is available. It's easy to go and buy Sambas in 52 different colours. In a way that's great but for me there was always a bit of a thrill in the chase and getting something that you really wanted and had to save up for. So, yeah, I still love shopping and I don't think that's ever going to change.

Steve White.

★ ★ ★

An interview with Paolo Hewitt. Paolo has written countless words on British youth culture and in this interview he speaks about where his passion for the subject came from.

It's 1963 and a young boy is humming and singing the words, 'She loves you yea, yea, yea' all day long. The young boy was a certain Paolo Hewitt, later known for his youth, football and Mod culture related books like *Beat Concerto, The Soul Stylist* and *The Fashion of Football*, to name just a few. The aforementioned Beatles song was Paolo's earliest memory of being captivated by music. The boy was five years old and I am certain he would have not been the first toddler to hum along to the Fab Four in the '60s.

At the time Paolo was living with his foster mother with whom he lived between the ages of four and ten years old before moving onto the Burbank Children's Home in Woking, Surrey. Paolo does, however, recall being awestruck by watching The Beatles on the London Palladium. As the years in the children's home rolled by and the small boy grew into his clothes so did his passion for music grow in his heart. This passion would later manifest itself alongside his other love. The other mistress was reading and writing. By the age of seven Paolo was submerging himself in what he termed 'Escapist books'. Examples of these books were *Treasure Island* and stories from Greek Mythology.

Paolo recalls a local shop owner would occasionally donate unwanted records to the children's home and because of this Paolo was exposed to a wide variety of musical genres. The Dubliners would get played in the home alongside the Woodstock album (a prized possession of his friend Colin who also lived in the home). Having access to many styles of music and many bands was a 'good education' says Paolo.

Other memories of the music of the day were Bowie's *Space Odditty*, a bit of Motown and a Faces album that 'got under' Paolo's skin. Everything about the album thrilled and excited him. The band members represented the kind of things that Paolo aspired to 'Fun, girls, freedom'. The album sleeve says it all. Several years later another boy from the neighbourhood called Paul Weller gave Paolo a tape cassette with six Small Faces [songs] recorded on it. In return Paolo gave Weller a tape with Faces songs. That is how Paolo discovered the Small Faces. He would later go on to write 'the young mod's forgotten story'.

By the time Paolo was attending St John the Baptist secondary school in 1971 the Brutus shirt, Loafers and Sta-Prest look of the Suedehead dominated the playground. Sadly Paolo was only getting two shillings pocket money a week so he was not in a position to buy the clothes he longed for. Paolo does recall sporting a tartan scarf that he loved which he wore in honour of Rod Stewart. Paolo remembers Pete, his mate from school arriving at school one day with a £40 Crombie on that his dad had bought him. The headmaster told the boy to go home. The boy went home only to return later with his angry father who gave the headmaster a bollocking ..and rightly so.

1971 meant the radios and local discos played Trojan alongside

Prog rock bands like E.L.P and Yes and then Bowie, Bolan and Roxy music. Paolo commented that he liked the early Genesis stuff and has fond memories of a song originally recorded by the Young Rascals and later by David Cassidy called 'How Can I Be Sure?'. Paolo also retold the story of the chatter in the playground the day after *Top of the Pops* showed Bowie put his arm around Mick Ronson during a performance of 'Starman'. The teenagers questioned the mystery of Bowie's sexuality. The shocking '70s eh! One day Paolo arrived at school with a copy of *Aladdin Sane* tucked under his arm. The headmaster considered the semi-naked body of Bowie to be offensive and inappropriate. This resulted in a three canning session from the head.

By the age of fourteen Paolo was an avid reader of *New Musical Express* (*NME*). 'The *NME* was my bible' remarks Paolo. He had also decided that writing was what he wanted to do and in 1978 enrolled in the North London Polytechnic to study English Literature. During this time he wrote for the student mag called *Fuse*. It was also around this time that Paolo returned to listening to the soul music of Motown and Stax. One night his search for soul led him to discover a small club near the Belsize tube station, with only twenty young people in it. The only music they played was soul on the type of labels that Paolo was listening to.

Paolo spent a large part of the '70s going to see bands like the Faces at Reading festival, which was 'a very disappointing' performance from his beloved band. He also saw The Who at the Valley which was, and still is, the home of Charlton Athletic Football Club. Paolo saw the Who again at Hammersmith Odean where they opened with 'I Can't Explain' and 'are still opening with it' he says. Paolo also nearly saw Led Zeppelin at Earl's court but he fell asleep three times. A local band from Woking called Squire also had gigs attended by Paolo. Squire would go on to be included in the list of the Mod revival of the late '70s.

Paolo says that he would go and see any band and would often frequent the Guildford Civic Hall on Sunday afternoon.

Additional to Paolo's list of bands seen were Dr Feelgood, Bob Dylan, the Rolling Stones and another Woking band with local lad's called the Jam. 'Music was my life blood, I was obsessed with music' says Paolo. This passion must have been evident because one of his teachers once said to him that 'if you knew as much about maths and English as you do music you would be Einstein'.

It was 1976 and Paolo was into the punk of the day. He wore Levi's jeans from Milletts and white tee shirt and looked like the Fonz from Happy Days. Paolo was listening to The Clash and the Sex Pistols. He remembers going into a local record shop called Aercos. He asked the girl behind the counter for a copy of 'Anarchy in the UK'. The girl collected the record and 'threw it on the counter in disgust'. This was why Paolo liked punk.

Paolo was just another boy about town and one day another young male called Enzo introduced him to one of his friends whose name was Paul Weller. Paolo would continue to see Weller around Woking and their relationship built up over the occasional nod and a 'you're alright, you're Enzo's mate'.

The Jam gigged their way around Woking and Paolo followed them around. One day Paolo entered a local pub called the Cotteridge. He spotted Weller sitting by himself. Paolo was faced with a dilemma, go and speak to him or avoid him. The problem was that only recently the Jam had been pictured on the front cover of his bible, the *NME*. Paolo thought if he talks to the lonely Weller he may think it's only because of *NME* but if he doesn't talk to him it could also be taken wrongly. In the end Paolo did speak to Weller and they spent the evening getting drunk together.

In 1979 Paolo, who was now living in London, got his first writing commission. It was a two hundred word piece for the *Melody Maker* on a Mod festival at The Marquee. Squire were amongst the bands performing. Paolo informed me that recently he rediscovered and read that article whilst doing some research for his latest book on the clothes the Beatles wore in the British

Library. So, Paolo started to get a wage. Now he had money to buy the clothes he had been deprived of during all those years living under the roof of children's homes.

Paolo's writing career progressed and he interviewed The Jam countless times and found a new job working for his bible of the past decade the *NME*. I for one spent my youth reading Paolo's words in that music mag. Paolo says the office was a strange place to be. It was an office with divided loyalties because of the music that the employees favoured and championed.

Throughout Paolo's youth he interviewed the likes of Marvin Gaye, Stevie Wonder and Nina Simone. Of Marvin, Paolo says when he interviewed him 'I didn't know my music' he referred to being too young (knowledgably) to really make the most of the opportunity. Of Nina he said he had to 'passed the test' before she would even allow him to interview her. Paolo owned twenty seven albums by her. He was clearly a massive fan and still is.

The interview continued with further discussion around music, bands, football (Paolo chose Spurs after telling himself that whichever team won the semi-final game between Spurs and Derby he would support. This was 1967) the Hip Hop of 85, Acid Jazz. I asked two more burning questions. I wanted to know what Paolo preferred leather shoes or suede shoes. He answered leather tongue and tassel loafers. When asked of a favourite shirt he said a blue and black tartan check Brutus that he once owned.

With that he gulped down his Peroni, I sipped my red wine and we both headed off in the directions of our required tube stations. On my journey home I reflected on the time spent with Paolo. It was a pleasure chatting with the man who evidently has a deep-rooted love for music and youth cultures. He knows his stuff.

With thanks to Paolo Hewitt, interviewed by Ian Snowball.

NORTHERN SOUL

Claire Russell, a late-bloomer who is now an obsessive.

Got into Mod/Northern Soul in 2001. I was a bit of a late bloomer, guess I moved around so much I was never really settled anywhere long enough and was always on the peripheral of things, ducking in and out of scenes as I evolved as a person.

But the music always appealed and filled my soul and heart every time I was lucky enough to hear its underground sound, somewhere, somehow by chance. It was like a big secret and fate seemed to be drawing me towards it.

I will never forget the first time I went to the 100 Club 6Ts all-nighter on Oxford Street. My first true foray into the scene. I was on a date that seemed fairly promising, he had mentioned the place and the music played and I was overjoyed to be able to get in to the inner sanctum at last – I was still fairly new to London and didn't know anybody, let alone know where to go. As I walked down the hallowed staircase, the muffled music got louder and clearer and my heart raced. I felt like I had found something so amazing and so special. I felt like, after all my travelling, I had at last found my home.

I looked around me in awe. The music, the feeling of togetherness… the dance moves! It was like discovering a new religion, and one I have been faithful to ever since… and always will be. I felt so bloody nervous and was afraid to dance – which went on for quite a few months until I started to suss what was going on and get my confidence up to get out on the floor. I met the fabled Keb Darge down there early on and asked him to teach me a dance move (being a fellow Scot we spoke the same language so I could be cheeky that way). Couldn't do it though, that man has some serious moves, meant only for him I think. I would be content with my basic four step shuffling for now.

It was weird for a while on the London scene around 2002/3, it all really quieted down for reasons I do not know to this day – perhaps everyone was avoiding me… aha! Maybe they all got into different music, I'm not sure. One night I got down there (the 100 Club) pretty late for an all-nighter, around 5 or 6 in the morning and there was only me, another bloke and and the DJ. It was really eerie but I hung on in there til the end, as did the DJ. You have to. It's just the way, dance till the absolute end. And the music is ALWAYS worth it. It's therapy after a hard week. It's finding yourself whilst simultaneously getting lost in the music.

I was into the Mod look at the time and there were a few Mods milling around the 100 Club, all congregating in what is affectionately known as Mod Corner to the left of the stage. I felt young there, even though I was already hitting 30. Some serious players in their '50s and '60s, direct from the original days of Northern Soul, still doing the mid-dance stretches then getting out there and spinning like tops before launching into athletic back drops. How could this be?! It was putting me to shame. Where were these dudes getting their energy?! A lot was pure love for the music and not just the drugs synonymous with the scene. It was incredible and I was permanently in awe.

At one point though I actually started to get seriously worried. Where were all the young dudes to keep the fire of Northern Soul blazing? At that point I wasn't travelling up to other do's around the country so wasn't really clued in on what was going on elsewhere. I mean they would all have to hang up their dancing shoes at one point, right? Shuffle off their mortal coils so to speak? Was Northern Soul going to die? I know it's morbid but I was so in love with the music that I was beginning to panic that it could all be over!

My fears were soon drop-kicked outta sight though as an influx of young Soulies shuffled on to the scene. The Wigan Young Souls emerged, all grown up now and with Soul in their genes. Elaine Constantine's film *Northern Soul* is out now, she trained lots of young dancers all the moves to make the film so authentic. They would be coming out to the clubs and the whole atmosphere re-charged. New nights were springing up everywhere and I started travelling to do's a helluva lot more. Sleeping on the train back after an all-nighter and feeling rather jet-lagged by Monday. I guess it's the closest I will ever get to the early days of Northern Soul, but I wish I could time travel and experience it for myself!

I have been into lots of different types of music – and I still am… but since Northern Soul my whole style of dance has changed. But that style… for me at any rate… with its basic four step shuffle can fit into any genre of music – I swear!

I have found my religion now. I believe. And I will FOREVER keep the faith.

Claire.

★ ★ ★

Pete McKenna, 'Once upon a Soul'.

Blackpool 72-73 and the whole world's a disco. Apprentice bricklaying at the time, freezing my bollocks off building the Crest Motel Preston five days a week with blokes I had nothing in common with. Three day weeks, strikes, power cuts – what the fuck's going on? Weekends on the disco merry go round on the piss pulling birds, scrapping with the hordes of grockles from pub to club to prom and back. Jingle bells jingle bells jingle all the way and all that bollocks. How can life be so crap for somebody so young? Searching for a way out, something different to do but when and where? It can't come quick enough, that I do know.

Starting to notice Lambrettas and Vespas everywhere and mates I know driving them, sheepskins, Levi's and Doc Martens. Looks like a well cool scene to get into and I feel an escape from Tinseltown is on the cards at last. A few weeks later and I'm in with them, The Okeh Scooter Crew with a brand new bog standard Lambretta GP125 courtesy of John Halls HP scheme. A discerning bunch of lads who don't suffer fools gladly, lads who go about their business different from the rest. A few weeks down the line and AFR539L is looking the business of a chair. Black paintwork, chrome side panels, crash bars, Bermuda backrest, Square Eight spot lamps with a 175cc barrel and piston fitted to give her some clout and sounding sweet. Great days out driving where we wanted to go in a squadron, sunshine, chrome mirror shades and no crash helmets to spoil the image.

Driving up to Cleveleys one Saturday night, walking into Gallopers and I immediately discover the music to fit the scene I'm now a part of. The one and only Pete Haigh behind the decks playing this music they call Northern Soul, a track by Jerry Williams called 'If You Ask Me' and I'm instantly hooked, rooted to the spot, listening to it. The vocals, the beat, the rhythm, like nothing I've ever heard before and I needed to hear more and fortunately didn't have to look too hard.

Unforgettable nights in The Peacock Room and Blackpool Casino with Bob Blackwood and the inimitable Baz Stanton – RIP gone but not forgotten – behind the decks. Great teachers to all the new students of Northern Soul. Sat nights up in Blackpool Meccas Highland Room with Ian Levine and the legendary Colin Curtis in charge of the music. So many people packed into such a small place, the passion and energy was unbeatable, meeting like-minded soulies from all parts of the country there for one reason. Nothern Soul and what a reason, what a scene as I finally waved goodbye to Tinseltown banality forever more. Rumours circulating around the scene of an old ballroom in Wigan with an all night license playing Northern Soul. Sounds too good to be true but what if?

Sunday soul sessions in Scoeys on Victoria Street reading a poster advertising a coach trip to Wigan Casino, places going fast and postal applications for membership accompanied by a stamped addressed envelope. Booked there and then and a week later, my membership's dropped through the letter box and I'm On My Way. All-nighter bags, towels, Brut, booze and Wrigleys wondering what will be waiting at the end of the line. An hour or so later, we're parked up outside this shabby Victorian ballroom that had seen better days but you can't judge a book by the cover, can you? Crowds of soulies standing around waiting for the witching hour, evil glares from a couple of stern looking skins, 'What the fuck are you lot doing here?' The same kind of looks we'd be giving strangers to the scene a few months later.

Walking into The Beachcomber for the first time, a narrow black tunnel lined with speeding eyes and not a pleasant sensation by any means. Into the main room that served as a garage in days gone by, a concrete lined hole with a DJ spinning sounds to dancing soulies while others sat around in groups, tea, coffee and Bovrils waiting for the main event. Seen nothing like it before, basic, rough but there was a great atmosphere – the lull before the storm kind of thing – and then we're outside in the queue crushed up tight, the Tuxedo doormen pulling in the animals two by two and we're in, memberships at the ready, up the stairs and the double doors leading to the main hall, full of expectation at what we were going to find.

The Devonnes 'Pick Up My Toys' was playing as we pushed open the thick plastic doors and walked into an unbelievable nocturnal world. A large dark hall packed full of soulies from all parts of the country, an ultra violet strip light hanging above the dance floor emitting a ghostly glow on the dancers below. People shuffling effortlessly from side to side, balanced and poised to perfection, stripped to the waist, baggies and leather soles shoes, spinning, back dropping, kicking and clapping, everyone doing their own thing but together in a unrehearsed choreography of dancing I'd never seen before, breathing in the smell of hundreds of bodies mixed with a hundred different deodorants. Breathtaking just watching the action from the wings, and up on the balcony, dealers buying and selling northern gems [records]. My first taste of a Wigan Casino all-nighter knowing I'd be back for more.

A few weeks down the line and my first chemical romance with black bombers, Filon, Blueys, Green and clears, Midnight Runners and Amphet powder tasting like cat piss – UGHH – but needs must. Energy pumping through me rapid as I joined the army of glaring eyes and bodies soaked in sweat. Staying in all week on the comedown, paying back what I'd borrowed from my body and then the weekend, always the weekend to look forward too. Cars, vans, trains and coaches arranged for the lift over making sure everyone had a place whether skint of not. Soulies in railway carriages dancing to portable cassettes on the last train to Wigan. Trying to keep warm in my mate's Rover Coupe, huddled around the heater waiting for the doors to open. Charnock Richard Motorway Services meeting up with mates from all over the place. Handfuls of gear in exchange for a few crumpled notes and change and off into the night once more.

Freezing cold nights wandering around Wigan, crowds dancing in the fish market warming up for the big one and always the coppers keeping their beady eyes open for people to bust. People clustered around and parked up in cars dealing gear, a nod, a handshake, a brief chat, a rummage through an inside pocket and sorted for the night. 'Cheers mate. See you next week. Have a good one'.

Hot sweaty nights greeted by ice cold mornings, walking back to the station crowded together in the waiting room freezing to death – 'Where's the fucking train then?' Exhausted, dreaming of a nice hot brew and a warm bed to crash into and the next weekend. Searching for soul, Saturday mornings, scooters parked up outside Sandy Mountains Symphonia record shop on Cookson Street. Inside packed out with sheepskins and Martens demanding records for their collections. Hundreds of singles lying around all over the place in some kind of orderly chaos and the learned Sandy standing there smiling, the font of all soul knowledge there to lend a hand. 'If you can't remember the title or the artist, just sing it or hum it and I'll find it for you'. Job done, bagged up and back home dying to put it on the stereo and practise a few moves before the big one. And Preston bus station, a young guy who knew a thing or two about northern operating from a small stall, picking up Temptations' 'Calling My Name' and 'Super Love' a few ahead of the crowd.

Why do all good things have to come to an end? The shock as the realisation kicked in that Wigan Casino had burned down, driving over to see for ourselves if the rumours were true and indeed they were. Just a smoking shell of unforgettable memories lay before our eyes parked up on the car park wondering what we were going to do next. Lou Pride, Dean Parrish, Dean Courtney, Phillip Mitchell, Rita Da Costa, Don Covay, Major Lance, Paul Anka, Williams and Watson, Johnny Bragg, Joe Hicks, NF Porter, Freddie Chavez, Judy Street, Christine Cooper, Brenda Holloway, Jimmy Radcliffe, Jimmy James, Case Of Thyme, Mirwood Strings,

Al Wilson, Frank Wilson. I could go on forever along with the memories, mistakes and regrets of a time and place in my life I am unable to forget so I'll leave you with the words of the immortal Tobi Legend. *Time Will Pass You By* and doesn't it just. Keep The Faith because at certain times in a person's life, faith is all we have left and believe me, I know all about that only too well.

Pete McKenna.

★ ★ ★

Bags, Spins and Soul memories from Will Vincent Hunt.

There's plenty been spoken and written about the history of the British soul scene, so despite decades of personal research, I won't try and recap with my own inaccuracies with who did what, where and when. This is purely a few snippets of my own experience, as I tried to personally recreate how it was, in the early '70s, in amongst an ever-changing scene.

I've been a skinhead since about Easter 1982, some years after the originals, but being born in '70s Sunderland gave me little choice. From musical beginnings, in ska and reggae (given a small helping hand by me and me brother Bob pinching me mam's collection of Blue Beat and Island 45s), apart from a few catchy Motown & Stax tunes, I hadn't shown a lot of interest in Soul, until I started attending Mod clubs in Newcastle. This was a relatively underground scene, mostly full of teenagers, but many with a passion for tailor-made suits, scooters and original '60s gems; mixed with a back drop of soul, R&B, Mowtown and ska, in a slightly cider-fuelled haze.

There was a great buzz, queuing outside of Mod all-niters, slyly checking the details on each other's clothes, eager to get on that dance-floor. I'd save my pocket money and dinner money (oh, how I was a hungry teenager!) to spend as much as possible on clothes and nights out. We'd scour second hand shops for original items and get the local tailor to do alteration work on old two tone suits (my pocket money certainly didn't extend to "bespoke"!) and sitting for hours sewing on cuff buttons and turning up trousers. I bought a pair of leather soled wingtip brogues from a shop in Hendon (best part of twenty quid – a lot of dinners missed), a pale imitation of the Cordovan lovelies I have now but I thought they looked the business at the time. If you shopped around Newcastle you could still get basket weave loafers, buckle riders and Hawkins Moon-hop 11 holers, and the charity shops were over flowing with Jaytex shirts and sheepskins for ten bob. I no longer fit into a 14" neck but I still wear most of the shoes I bought back then.

We'd often head off of a weekend, crammed into one of the older lad's cars, off to some grim town in Yorkshire or Lancs for a pure soul niter. I will never forget six of us squeezed into a beat up Ford Fiesta (I'd love to say Ford Anglia, but it was 1986!), none-stop soul in the cassette player, destination The Twisted Wheel in Manchester – still at the original Whitworth Street venue (as it is today). It was the club's monthly night off from Rocky's [gay] club... The venue had changed little since its hallowed late '60s days (from what I'd been told). No massive dance-floor like many clubs of the time, but a few smaller rooms in a dingy basement – not a pretty sight. But the atmosphere was intense, and as the night went on, the sweat rained down from the low slung ceilings. My only regret from the night was getting ready at home thinking that a good choice of footwear would be my new riders which I'd previously hammered about 40 segs into each sole. A shiny wooden floor smeared with beer, sweat and talc didn't often agree with a full set of Blakeys, if ye wanted to risk more than a (Harlem) shuffle. I remember some old bloke (probably in his early-30s) shaking my hand and chuckling summet to his mate like, 'Ahh – look at the little skinhead'. I did look very young for my years back then! The strange thing is, even now at niters 20-odd years later, I look around and I'm still one of the youngest there.

I'd often head off to Keale with a mate Little Micky, niter bag over me shoulder with a small towel and a bottle of Brut, long before we had our own transport, walking miles to the station, a coach to Manchester, bus to Stoke, another bus to Keale and a walk through the campus. Must have been almost a full day's travel either way. After a quick change in the toilets, we'd endure what seemed like marathon dance sessions, then scrounge a lift into Stoke and spend hours on buses long after the excitement had all worn off. Always back for more though as the music, friends, atmosphere all made it worth-while.

Spins
There's always been a manoeuvre on the dance-floor that ye can do, or ye can't… and that's spin. This first became apparent at our regular Tuesday night spot, The Wreck; I watched as two old soul boys had a spin-off against each other to Junior Walker's Tune Up' (still probably my favourite Motown tune).

Always a tryer, I've been spinning for years, mostly unsuccessfully. For me (and I'm sure plenty of others), there's that moment when you carry off what seems like a perfect spin and an air of smug satisfaction washes over you, leaving a grin lasting at least till the end of the record. Then there's the other 90% of times when you spin off like a top across the floor, banging into people along the way (it's often a good job the Soul dance-floor etiquette allows such misdemeanours without a fight breaking out as it often would elsewhere).

My 'worst spin of all time' has to be in the soul room on the Isle of Wight, some years back when I went into a massive spin, through what seemed to be a black hole in space and time. I landed flat on me back, looked up and all I saw was nothing. Everyone had gone; the thumping beat had disappeared and I was staring at a dark ceiling. For a moment I was totally confused.

Had I been asleep? Had the do finished and I was on my own, still on the dance-floor? Then a big door swung open and large bouncer figure held out his hand, frowning with disdain. Apparently, I'd spun across the floor, through some double doors, into another room, so by the time I landed the doors had swung closed, shutting out any evidence of where I was supposed to be. So I am genuinely jealous of those you see on the floor, spinning effortlessly for what seems forever. Cap doffed.

Oxford bags
Clothes have always been a big part of being a skinhead for me. A recreation of the original styles with an attention to detail and authenticity. From the work boots, rolled up Levi's and braces look that came out of '60s mod, through the check Bennies, toniks, Crombie's and beyond, I've always been, what can only be described as obsessed, recreating looks from the whole era, through to suedehead, smoothie & soul boy. As trousers started to get wider in 1971-72, straight leg Levi's Sta-Prest evolved to parallels, waistbands thickened and Oxford bags (or Birmingham or Brummie bags) emerged. A million variations on a theme came and went, but the bags were common place in the soul clubs of the north, like the Torch, Catacombs and later onto Wigan.

Now I know I was in nappies when all this was going on, but I've had me fair share of parallels over the years. 2, 3, 4, 5 button waistbands, multiple pockets, crown flaps, leg pockets, buttons galore and sometimes enough fabric to sail a ship. In the true spirit of youthful one-up-manship, "biggest is best" often prevailed (as it did, at times with biggest sideboards, most mirrors on your Lambretta, most ticket pockets or cuff buttons on yer suit etc etc.). I was at a scooter rally, late one night, arguing with an old mate, Dosser about who had the biggest pair of oxford bags. I had some 18 pocket, high waisted 32 inchers at the time (bought in Aflecks on me way to Keale), so confidently argued my point. So we agreed that when we met up next, we'd settle the score. I'd heard through the grapevine a few weeks later that he'd been to the tailor and had a pair of 36 inch parallels knocked up especially.

With no time to see a tailor myself, and never wanting to be outdone, what choice did I have? So off to the fabric shop at the weekend to get some supplies. Having never made a pair of trousers before, it was a little daunting, so asked the advice of the shopkeeper. I picked out some suitable black cloth … "I'm making a pair of trousers and need some help," I said. So we went through outside leg measurements etc. "They'll be quite wide – about 40 inches at the bottom," I continued. "No problem," she muttered as she measured it out. "And there'll be a few pockets" … bit more fabric … "and some buttons – 72, so give me 80 just in case". The woman never raised a smile the whole time. So, with me mother's '60s Jones sewing machine, I set to work, with tailor's chalk and optimism. My first attempt of a waist-band and fly wasn't too professional, but after a re-think and what must have been every night for a fortnight, beavering away like Rumplestiltskin, they were done. It was Bridlington Scooter rally (89 I think), and it was one of those moments when I walked into a very crowded pub, the place went silent and everyone looked round with gasps of horror and amusement. Me mate turned up in his newly crafted strides but they were no match for my home-made efforts – 16 button waistband, 22 pockets, 72 buttons and 42 inch parallel legs were enough to win any prize. I still wear them now, but I've since learnt how there's a trick to getting down stairs without falling down them and how to piss in the gents without filling up ye turn-ups.

While I'm on about bags, I found an old '70s tailored pair once with about 48 petal flaps, too many buttons to count and a good 40 inch straight leg. I took them away with me to a soul week in the Canaries. First night on, I then noticed that the zip catch was bust and it wouldn't stay up. So I carefully safety pinned them from the inside, then off to the do. My first trip to the toilet meant fiddling on with my safety pin for ten minutes, a rigmarole

I knew couldn't continue. Next time in, I realised that the trousers were so baggie I could roll up the leg and simply piss out of one side. This did get me a few funny looks later when there were no spare cubicles.

It will be a sad shame when the original crowd finally hang up there favourite leather soles and the scene disappears. There are a few youngsters around, which is refreshing to see – not just nightclub tourists, but genuine soul fans, often leaving me green with envy as they handstand and fly around with the exuberance of youth firmly on their side. But the core has always (in my time) been the old crowd who were there at the Casino and beyond. Hopefully by the time it disappears, I'll be too old to backdrop (is there such an age?!) and will have banked enough memories to bow out gracefully.

After 20 odd years of niters and soul dos, I've met a lot of good friends; chewed a lot of Wrigley's; lost a lot of weight (I think 9lb in one night was my record); ruined a few pairs of shoes (I danced the leather sole clean off a pair of Solatios one night, leaving me trying to dance on an insole and a few nails); talked a lot of rubbish (and listened to a lot more); split a few pairs of trousers; showed off (and been showed up); danced in the isles while Junior Walker wandered, blowing his sax, amongst the appreciative crowd; suffered various minor injuries; I've grabbed a couple of hours kip after a long night of dancing, before riding me Lambretta home, bleary eyed and dehydrated (mind you, that was about 2 years ago); I've danced to records that made my hair tingle, made me laugh, made me cry.

But for now, I'm still dressing like it's 40 years ago, still riding Lambrettas and still making the most of the thriving scene that eases the opportunity to never grow up. All in all I'm pleased and proud to have played my part in what has to be the coolest underground music scene in existence. Long may it continue?

Will Hunt Vincent.

* * *

A '90s Skinhead with a passion for Soul music. Matty Morris.

When I was greatly younger I remember my days with family down the local working men's club. Seeing my uncles and friends dress in skinhead outfits and lace up there 10 holers and dance to Madness and Two Tone. There were different groups back then. Rock and rollers, new age romantics. Never any aggro, just groups getting ready to dance there jig to their delegated time slot. I suppose I was so young. My child roots had been breakdancing, another classic of the day. However, with my ability to learn break dancing fairly quickly and then to change dances to rock and roll and then swing to Madness and songs like 'Driving In My Car' stood me in good stead for the future.

My mum and dad were ex-skins, my dad even an ex-mod; however, I don't remember any of that, only that I hated a red gingham check shirt that was soon to become one of my favourite shirts as a child and the monkey boots and flight jackets and the hand-me-down Fred Perrys from all my cousins to my brother to me. My dad was an ex-skin DJ from the local area so maybe the music was going to wear off on me unknowingly. My mum was more subtle, disco and Marvin Gaye, Tamla Motown. You could say I had a varied musical background.

Northern Soul and the Scootering Scene started back in the day between leaving school and starting college 1992. Not long after getting my first scooter which was a dream of mine for half a year since getting in to the mod scene (me and my mates) via the great classic film *Quadrophenia* and the *Scootering* mag. A strange time to be getting into the scene. Music was dead for us in the charts and our escape was old music. A few of my mates saw a club scooterist do (The Medway SC) going on so we decided to go. I can remember some guy saying, "Who are you lot supposed to be?" I replied, "The reincarnation of the mods," to which he laughed and walked on. Not knowing the scene then as I do now. We loved the mixture of sounds and heard and saw a kind of dance unknown. We wanted to dance but it looked so alien. We loved the music. It seemed familiar to soul and motown yet different. Anyway we tried. I can remember saying to my mates, "Take the piss". Just dance and you will be doing it. We were all movers and somehow taking the piss or letting go we were pulling it off. Or we thought we were?

It felt good to let go and find a crowd of like-minded people. A few months later I happened by chance to come across a couple of Scooterists. More Scooter Boy and Girl. With a passion for scooters and Northern Soul. I was already greatly involved with old/vintage music from my childhood. It was their passion and guidance on music and record labels and giving me duplicates that they had bought that I started off. Of course going to boot fairs and rifling through old 45s and albums and comparing our finds. I obviously came off worse in terms of knowing Northern Soul records.

Time progressed Rallies, runs, Scooterist Northern Soul. Many great adventures. I got married; my wife fell pregnant and gave birth to my daughter bought a house, moved house. Pretty much a scootering life. That is until Camber Sands rally kicked the scene from Northern connoisseurs to open top blow you away all-night dancing. That was the case for me anyway. My passion to dance to scooterist Northern Soul as I call it had been going a while. However, the scene was a vibrant dance floor of Northern Soul, Skin, Punk, Mod and Indie all in one room. As fantastic as all this was (drinking, dancing, taking the pi**) the all-nighters of Camber seemed to take me over. No longer was I doing the scooterist side. I was now going from Northern Soul to Reggae rooms. By now I was and had a been a skinhead for while since 96. Clothes became baggier, Jaytexs were being worn again by a scene springing up. Hair longer, less macho some would say. It has a new feeling but old in essence. They looked and classed themselves as old... Maybe I had only just discovered it. Maybe I was part of creating the new look and passion within a small band of Northern Soul dancers from the skinhead world. These people were very like-minded and sprung from the bad old days of youths finding their feet and not tolerating other youth group's gangs or musical tastes.

The scootering scene had whipped this up and shown the best of all cults. Perhaps we were a generation younger, more tolerant, that had enjoyed so many different musical passions that a new subculture was going to be born. Very similar to Suedehead but a generation schooled on so much diversity and musical talents that to discover Northern Soul culminated this in a new generation wanting all night dancing to something we loved and related to. Something that although we had not heard directly, it had influenced our childhood music. Of the '80s and '90s where everything seemed to be a remix of old. This was Northern Soul and I think the birth for me of the Soul Skin. Not a big group of people. On the fringes, you see them, smart and shuffling. Someone influenced by Northern Soul with roots firmly in Reggae and the Skinhead way of life. But with passion and love of soul and dancing and partying hard. Somehow Camber made the Soul Skin for me.

My life in the scooterist scene had been going for a while when Camber started and I was an established shuffler. However, I left the comps and bigger move dancing to a chosen few. Camber introduced me to the Northern Soul Competition. Some would argue it isn't a proper comp. However, I disagree, the amount of people entering from a shuffle to a somersault has grown and is growing. Bigger than some national dance comps.

I remember on an occasion when a friend finally striked up enough bravado to attempt Northern Soul dancing. After having a deep conversation with him he walked across the dance floor and started dancing only to realise it was in fact the change in record for the dance final. To which the DJ unceremoniously shouted at him to leave the floor. Thankfully it didn't deter him and he was shuffling about in the future. I did say to him fair play for attempting your first Northern Soul dance in a comp final. I said he had big bollocks for that!!! Lol.

Scootering was a must but more was needed. Camber had kicked off a dancing passion. I was in a transition from scootering to Northern Soul. I started to attend the breakaway scootering movement that had started to do dedicated soul dos once again. The odd soul do was taken in around London, South Coast and Essex. I was loving the music. New records, unheard of from my prospective. That's the thing about Northern Soul, in 18 years of discovering it, I am still finding and hearing records at do's on CD compilations, it's amazing.

Matty Morris.

PSYCHOBILLY

*DMs, Me and Psychobilly by Alan Wilson,
The Sharks & Western Star Records.*

I have worn Dr. Martens for the last 42 years of my life. I can still
remember getting my first pair. I used to lust after DM boots in
a boot shop window in Lawrence Hill, Bristol. I managed to get
my dad to come look at them. He wasn't keen as this was the
skinhead era and he felt them not suitable for an impressionable
kid. However, the salesman did a great job and sold the idea of
plenty of ankle support to a boy who would be running crazy
in the streets and climbing trees etc. The clincher was when my
father turned the boot over and read the words "Oil, Acid and
Petrol resistant" etc. I felt like a king in my 8-holed cherry red
boots and still get a real buzz out of buying DMs.

In my teens I got into '50s Rock and Roll music (this was
by now the mid-late '70s). Whilst I often sported creepers and
winklepickers, my DMs were still in almost daily use. Thankfully
for me, an offshoot from the Rockabilly scene called Psychobilly
happened in the very early '80s. I was there at the sharp end (and

have been with it ever since).This new genre took elements of its look from both the Rockabilly & Punk image and my DMs were now more important than ever to me and my own personal dress code.

I've somehow managed to make a career as a musician and DMs are part of my trademark look. I still wear DMs (normally steel toe caps) everywhere. I wear them onstage all over the world when performing with my bandThe Sharks. People always remark on them! Psychobilly has become an important part of my life and DMs have been an integral part of my life in the Psychobilly world. It's amazing how every subculture has embraced DM's over the decades, not least the Psychobilly scene. I've been part of the Psychobilly movement since before it had a name and DM's are an essential part of mine and the whole genre's wardrobe.

About four years ago I was recording *The Infamy* album for my band The Sharks, and I needed a 'creaking' sound at the start of the song 'Ship To Shore'. So I actually mic'd up my boots and recorded the sound of the leather creaking as I flexed my feet. The boots worked perfectly.

Alan Wilson.

★ ★ ★

Richard Smith offers a first-hand account of the early days of Psychobilly.

In 1981, I was 15, and I started going to a club in Southgate, north London called The Royalty. At the time it was known as 'The home of Rock 'n' Roll' hosting the likes of Carl Perkins, The Everly Brothers and one of the last gigs that Bill Haley ever played. It was a real hot bed for Teddy Boys, Rockers and the new up and coming Neo Rockabilly's. It was most famous for having the balcony that Jimmy dives off of in *Quadrophenia*.

Rockabilly was having a revival, new bands popping up everywhere. The Polecats, The Blue Cats and The Deltas all bought out records and played at The Royalty, we all bopped along to all of them. Then one day the DJ played a song that was slightly different, it wasn't about Thunderbirds or Pink peg slacks, it was about Voodoo and it really rocked! I went and asked the DJ and he said it was a band called The Meteors.

The next time the DJ played the song, two or three blokes got up and started jumping around, pushing each other over, and everyone just stared unbelieving at what we had just seen. I thought to myself, *I must buy this record to find out what all the fuss is about*. I saved my money up and bought it from Rex's record stall upstairs at The Royalty. When I came down everyone asked me what I had bought, and when I told them they grumbled and told me I should have bought Gene Vincent or Johnny Burnette!! *Hmm*, I thought, *this is upsetting people*. I took it home and played the A side with 'Voodoo Rhythm' and 'Maniac Rockers', but when I flipped the disc to the B side and heard 'My Daddy is a Vampire' then 'You Can't Keep a Good Man Down', I thought, *This is really different!*

Then on July 29th there was a royal wedding and we all got a day off school, The Royalty put on a "special cats nite out" with White Lightnin', The Fantoms and headlining The Meteors. I got ready in my suit and tie and headed off to The Royalty. Right from the outset it was obvious that the people turning up that night weren't from the usual rockin' crowd.

White Lightnin' and The Fantoms came and went and then The Meteors took the stage, there was no trendy '50s gear just boots, jeans, donkey jackets and no tops! Not seen at The Royalty before!

There was a tradition at the Royalty that when the bands played the girls in their pretty dresses would stand on chairs in a semi-circle so they could see the band, and tonight was no exception. The Meteors picked up their instruments and Nigel Lewis the bass player shouted, "GO MENTAL!" and the crowd did, knocking every girl off their chair. It carried on like that, all night, fights between Psychobillies and Teds were starting up all over the place, Paul Fenech the guitarist spat chicken blood out while Nigel Lewis sang 'My Daddy is A Vampire'.

It was a gig I will always remember for more than one reason; it was the last time I wore a suit and when I started listening to punk/psychobilly bands more. Later I bought their album, a friend of mine told me they had it in Our Price and I went in twice not finding it, until it dawned on me that it wasn't in the Rockabilly section, it was under 'M'. A new genre had begun.

Richard Smith.

★ ★ ★

'A Postcard from Brighton – Wish You Were Here' by Anne-Marie Krolick.

"It's criminal," my mum cried, with real tears starting to well up...

"How could they do that to your beautiful hair?"

Job done! My first flat-top haircut got exactly the reaction I had hoped for!

Thanks to Freddy's, the barber shop who virtually single-handed sculpted the subcultures of Brighton, I was ready for a summer of psycho-fun in the seaside sun. Smelling not-so-subtly of 'hard rock hairspray' and cheap washing up liquid (what exactly was in that clear bottle of 'Freddy's lotion'?) I hit the beach...

Back then is was quite simple; if you were different you were 'IN' Punks, Mods, Metal-heads, Skaters, Skins, Goths whatever as long as you could stomach continuous 'On Blueberry Hill' and were the sworn enemy of 'the West Street Casuals' you were welcome at the Belvedere.

Through my rose-tinted (fake) Ray Bans I can still see the Black Mambas shine, plastic beacons of iridescent purple; alcoholic rocket fuel for a beach scene of laughing, flirting, chatting and the occasional ruckus. A new soundtrack drifts in; move over Fats, it's time for the kids to take over 'Bottle on the Beach', 'Rumble in Brighton', 'Endless Sleep' establishing this new Psychobilly scene with old rockin' beats but brimming with teenage attitude manifesting itself in testosterone fuelled, sweat dripping wreckin' pits. Every weekend there was a new band to discover; the self-proclaimed kings of the scene The Meteors, über-slick Guana Batz, mayhem with King Kurt, pretty boys Restless in their PJs, The Richmond, The Old Vic, whatever the venue, always packed out and always with the Texans in support. This was pre-ecstasy, pre-Red Bull, pre-drum machines and with no need for a DJ to spell out the obvious, we knew we were, 'Right Here, Right Now!'

Was it history in the making? We neither knew nor cared. The future went only as far as the next weekend, the past didn't exist, with no internet to haunt us, thank f★★k no Facebook with its eternal self-absorbing posterity.

It's easy to look back and idealise the past, who doesn't want to remember themselves from a snapshot of their youth; with no responsibilities, unrestricted by time with the summer stretching endlessly ahead. It's wonderful to think back over those faces (some now sadly missed), all fresh, tanned, glossy haired, like Dorothy emerging over the rainbow all sugar dipped in Technicolor against a sepia seaside postcard whispering enticingly 'Wish You Were Here'.

But this is Summer in Brighton so of course it starts to rain and although the sturdiest quiffs may survive the downpour, the rose-tinting washes out of this picture. As I refocus I can see in the shadows a darker side, a constant undercurrent of menace fuelled by racism, homophobia, xenophobia, sexism and casual violence. There's a very fine line between boisterous fun and aggressive hedonism and as with any pack mentality that line got crossed regularly.

So I'm glad I'm not there, I don't need to go back, though my liver can't cope with Snakebite anymore and the sun gave me wrinkles. I don't have the time or inclination to spend an hour a day on my hair and make-up! Psychobilly has survived, it's still Here, still Now, no need to live in the past, there's a new generation of bands to discover, new faces to meet, but now the scene is wiser, more equal, more tolerant ... and the Long Tall Texans are still busking in Churchill Square!

Anne-Marie Krolick.

★ ★ ★

Little Jo, renowned Psychobilly expert and founder of the seminal Alcoholic Rats website.

I loved music from a very young age, originally influenced by my parents' love of '50s Rock n Roll and then a varied diet of chart stuff throughout the '70s and early '80s; glam rock, punk, indie, 2Tone, mod, etc. I went to my first gig at 13, the start of something that would stay with me for a lifetime.

On leaving school I got myself a Vespa and took on the lifestyle that would have me travelling up and down the country attending Scooter Rallies of a weekend. The Rallies had started off predominantly mod but by the mid-80s they were attended by Scooterists with a variety of musical persuasions. It seemed that pretty much anything went: Northern Soul, punk, ska and psychobilly were all catered for. This suited my musical tastes perfectly as I loved it all, but by now my foot was firmly set in the Psychobilly camp.

As well as going on rallies I had been attending The Klub Foot and other psychobilly gigs on a regular basis for some time; going to see bands like Guana Batz, The Stingrayz, The Cramps, The Meteors, etc.

The image was an all-important part of the psychobilly youth cult, particularly the hair. Like the scooterist, the staple wardrobe was mainly jeans (bleached), boots and white cut-off t-shirts depicting all your favourite bands, and checked shirts usually obtained from Millets. Footwear was generally Dr Martens, Monkey Boots, Deck shoes, Mocassins or Creepers. Dragging influences from the hillbilly days, dungarees were very much in vogue. Leather jackets were painted with the colourful graphics of band logos. 1950s style college baseball jackets were worn although these tended to be replicas rather than the originals with leather sleeves, unless you were very well off and could afford the likes of the prices charged in retro secondhand markets. Chunky knitwear in the form of argyle or grandad style jumpers and cardigans were popular, as were ski jumpers. Girls wore the same as the fellas but occasionally opted for a mini skirt or kilt – still worn with boots. Saying that, some of the fellas wore kilts too so it could definitely be stated that the style was unisex.

The hair had to be most time-consuming pastime of any self-respecting psychobilly. Bleached or coloured flat tops, quiffs and mohicans all standing proud, held in place with Shockwaves gel and Insette spiky hairspray, shaved bald or grade one at the side.

One of the few bands that I hadn't seen was King Kurt despite owning their records. Luckily I was invited to a local Scooterist's (Emmett RIP) surprise 18th birthday party where his family had arranged for his favourite band to play at his party. It was a great night where I got to see a band that would become one of my favourites for the rest of my life. The King Kurt boys were a good bunch, they didn't hide away in dressing rooms or clear off once they'd played, they stayed and partied with us which no doubt went a big way to them becoming a firm favourite at rallies and gigs for years to come. That, and the fun element that was always a huge part of their shows.

From then on I went to see King Kurt many times over the years. You never knew quite what you were going to get, except a good night guaranteed with lots of fun and mess. They really lived up to the moniker "The Masters of Mayhem". Their gigs were a unique experience with the band dressing up in all matter of costumes, extreme hairstyles, flour and eggs being thrown about all over the shop, and buckets of oozing gunk being poured over people's heads and shared with the audience during the snakebite drinking contests.

It was through this association with King Kurt that our all-girl scooter club came about. As we were all fond of a little tipple, their song 'Alcoholic Rat' struck a chord. I drew up a t-shirt design of the rat sprawled out on a scooter donning a bottle of vodka, but asked Maggot if he would draw it up properly. Being the artistic one of the band he did a fine job, it was so in keeping with all the other King Kurt t-shirts that the band sold themselves. Maggot introduced me to Russ the guy who printed up and sold the band t-shirts at The Klub Foot, and before long we were the proud owners of our own King Kurt inspired club t-shirts and called ourselves the Alcoholic Rats Scooter Club.

Adulthood came along and I stopped gigging in the early '90s when I had my children. I lost touch with the live scene for nearly a decade but never stopped loving the music. The internet was just coming about in the 2000s and I was constantly googling old psychobilly bands to see if anything was still happening. As luck would have it one of my searches came up that my other favourite band, the Guana Batz, were playing in London that night. It was great see them again and get that same old buzz. Older and wiser maybe but being in front of that stage took me back to being a teenager again. Later that year we also got to see I Can't Believe It's Not King Kurt at Woolacombe Rally. Smeg and his backing band performed a short set of classics to an army of old scooterbillies wearing grass skirts and stick-on quiffs – time hadn't been kind to those hairlines. But it was the welcome return of me doing what I loved best, going to live shows again.

As there was little on the internet about psychobilly, I decided to set up my own website to write reviews and share the photos that I took at rallies and gigs. Before long it had sections dedicated to King Kurt, Guana Batz and a gig guide – of course it had to be named Alcoholic Rats. Twelve years on and I'm still going to as many gigs as I can, I'm still loving my old favourite bands as well as a whole load of new talent that has hit the scene and I'm still running web pages for King Kurt, Guana Batz and the UK Psychobilly Gig Guide. I hope it continues for many more years to come!

Little Jo.

PUNK

Damien Wilson — On how punk influenced him in his childhood… and has done so ever since.

When I was really young, say 5 or 6, I was watching the TV and I saw Bowie on there, the whole Ziggy Stardust look, orange haircut, make-up flashes across his face. As I got a little older, I was thinking, *Glam or punk? Punk or glam?* I actually think the crossover there is quite strong, early punks looked like glam rock, no difference in my opinion, New York Dolls and all that. Look at the early Sex Pistols. Pretty much that look. I think before it was called punk, there was a vibe that something was going on that was a bit edgy, that you couldn't quite grasp, and people didn't understand it. I thought that was quite alluring even at a young age. That stayed with me and influenced me through my early childhood because I felt like I needed to stand out, not when I was 5 or 6 but when I was 12, and into my teens. As I got older, that stayed with me.

Before this, everyone was wearing flares and shitty t-shirts and riding round on bikes with no saddles, it was that sort of time. My biggest influence back then was my godmother Francis. My parents were hippies in the '60s, we lived in Ladbroke Grove and she was my mum's best friend. She was a rock photographer and used to hang around with bands, she was on the early punk scene but before that she was involved with that pub rock scene, like Kilburn and the High Roads. She was good mates with Ian Dury, for example, and she got me his album *New Boots & Panties*, which was a real influence on me. She knew Elvis Costello, Hawkwind, all these bands and she hung out and went on tour with them. She was very influential on me, she was around all these bands and was massively enthusiastic, so she became a bit of a litmus for me to what was going on. She was very much my connection to what was going on.

I didn't really know of the Sex Pistols at the time they were actually happening, I didn't really know they existed in the late '70s, no way. I was too young. However, Francis introduced me to those sort of ideas. For example, she got me a very weird sort of jacket, I was about ten at the time and it was like almost a New Wave style, with grey and lightning stripes in it (I've still got it now). I dunno where she got it from, it was a bit odd, but I really liked it – the thing about punk in its essence is it should be about individuality, but in a way what happened often was quite the opposite of that. So my early experiences were behaving like I wanted to look different to other people, very much that, so I used to wear that jacket and I managed to get myself a studded wrist band from one of those thousands of alternative little shops.

Then I got a camo jacket about 1980 from a military surplus store, which is where a lot of punks used to shop at the time. Then I think my parents bought me a pair of Dr. Martens when I got to secondary school, around 1981. When I got there, everybody started to get educated – or though they were educated – about what sort of subculture they wanted to be involved in. It was very diverse. You had the Casuals starting to appear, who in my experience weren't really called Casuals at the time, but they were wearing Diadora and ski jackets, stuff like that; then you had New Romantics; then you had your proper punks with Mohicans, we started to get all that; then we had skinheads who crossed over with the punk thing and then that crossed over into the Mod thing, which started developing into the scooter boy thing, with Lambrettas and Vespas. That was all ticking along, everyone was in their little cliques. You had to belong to one clique but then you might make a change and those changes could be quite drastic!

I stuck with the punk thing, though. We went to live in Brighton and a mate of mine moved to Harrow but we stayed in touch and then after a while we met up, and we were both wearing exactly the same leopardskin t-shirt with the sleeves cut off and little studded bracelets! Not many kids were wearing those at that point, well, not at ten year olds at least. That's what punk did to us. It infected us.

By 12/13, people started to think, *You are either one thing or another.* I'd decided I wanted to be a punk so that meant going down the route of getting my ears pierced, getting a Mohican, which gradually appeared. I didn't just go out and get it shaved on, it was cut at the sides and longer at the top at first, then gradually it became the full bore, dyed black, full Mohican.

One thing that really did influence me was going to a mate's house in Harrow and there was a picture of Sid Vicious with his top off on a motorbike, that was a turning point, I just thought that was brilliant. Then I listened to the Sex Pistols and stuff, everybody said if you were a punk you had to have *Never Mind The Bollocks.* That period was interesting because music-wise, if you think about it, after that, about 82, punk moved into this quite angry, very angry in fact, phase, things like Exploited, Anti-Nowhere League, and that's where I was at when I was younger, and it was pretty heavy duty at times.

Another thing about punks was that in my experience there were never big groups of punks roaming around, like you'd get gangs of skinheads. You'd probably have just a few punks in each village. I remember going on holiday to St Ives when I was about 15 and there was this scene of people who would congregate on the sea front where you'd end up with people from different parts of the country all into punk, because there just weren't many people doing that at the time. There weren't even that many magazines specifically for punk, there was *Sounds* and *NME* etc, but no real punk magazines, apart from the fanzines. There wasn't a punk newspaper that everybody read.

Back then, there were all these groups of people looking for an identity, looking for people to hang around with, searching for groups of people that were supposed to be individual but in a sense ended up being exactly the fucking same. That's not what punk was supposed to be about. It just became manufactured. To be fair, when you are young, you want to look different but then again you want to find a group of people that you can identify with, so there's a paradox.

However, I can't underestimate the influence of punk on my life and attitudes. I think it's fair to say that once punk has interested or influenced you, it doesn't ever really leave you. The problem with punk was that it ended up getting called punk – the *spirit* of punk was great. Before knowing what it was called, I remember thinking, *This is great, it's creative and shocking and different. It makes you stand out from the crowd. Don't do what the mainstream wants you to do.* Now *that's* the point of punk.

Damien Wilson.

★ ★ ★

'Punk Rock done by our sens' by Tony Beesley.

For me and my mates, punk was all about creativity and do-it-yourself. The attitude and music came first, but then a visual reflection of those had to be devised. Us young band of punk pups arrived after the summer of 77, so while our older pals were going to see early gigs by The Clash, The Jam and The Adverts, we were tuning into the Boomtown Rats, Stranglers and The Jam at the youth club disco... but we also meant it, maaan!!!

The first job at hand was to get my shoulder-length '70s hair cut to a Paul Weller styled short and spikey cut, followed by tight-fitting Adidas tops, white tennis shoes and my old Brutus jeans flares being chopped down a size or two. We were young, naïve and ill-informed but it was our teenage revolution! Next came the Bowie pegs, a lime-green mohair jumper that my Mum knitted me and would never stop growing. Jam shoes were worn for a while as were combat trousers, donkey jackets and Denis the Menace striped jumpers, pvc trousers, cheap plastic jackets and an increasingly dishevelled hair style. Punks? Our version was more like an outbreak of Dickensian street urchins on the rampage than your average bondage-suited Kings Road photo-friendly Punk Rocker!

The atypical punk look did make an appearance, though. Trying to copy our older punk brethren, with zip-covered jeans, torn t-shirts and leopard print shirts, but after making a few trips to trendy punk boutique, X-Clothes in Leeds and seeing the prices (I only ever bought one item – a pair of bus conductor trousers to wear to school and annoy the teachers), I soon opted for the real D.I.Y expression of punk. I painted my Doc Martens boots bright yellow, made my own Clash-imitation shirts with zips, Clash patches and stencilled slogans on the back, created my own badges, re-cycled old black fluffy jumpers with splatters of model paint on them, old school ties and the obligatory torn school blazer.

When we finally got to join the older punk flock to see bands like the Stranglers, The Clash, The Damned, 999 and The Jam, we were in awe of the real punks from the city. Bandsman's jackets, blue-suede shoes, coloured jeans and real Clash styled shirts for the lads, pvc, rubber, tiger print shirts and panda eye make-up for the girls, Johnny Thunders look-a-likes, every colour of hair imaginable and attitudes to match. We were punk midgets in Buzzcocks and Rezillos t-shirts, scared and nervous as hell but we joined in and soon became as seasoned as the old guard. It wouldn't be long before it was all over, as far as I was concerned, though. As clichéd as it sounds, Punk did become a uniform and I was not gonna be part of a regimented correctly-uniformed tribe. On my first few sightings of mohawks and crusty old glue and cider-saturated punks, I was out for good. My Mod sensibilities that were always there during punk came back to the fore and, whilst I retained my punk attitude and idealism permanently, I never went out in a pair of pvc trousers and a mohair jumper again. Neither did I embrace the mod revival as I wasn't going to swap one tribe for another, more-over I took what I liked from Mod, Punk and other styles and moved ahead into the '80s!

Tony Beesley.

★ ★ ★

Bruce Brand, on early punk gigs and music.

1977, I was at college with Billy (Childish) and Russ Wilkins. Russ was our kind of guiding light in those days and it was him who introduced us to punk rock. I went out and got The Clash's first album, The Damned, The Jam and the Sex Pistols. At the time all those bands' first albums were brilliant. Some of the punk bands' second albums were more dreary and this was very much the general consensus at the time. But the first Clash album had so many good songs on it.

Then after getting those first albums I started listening to more '60s music. Punk and those albums were like a catalyst for me. I mean, before punk came along I was stuck listening to the generic rock sound of the time… like Led Zeppelin and Status Quo. But even when punk rock came along I still decided to carry on liking what I like and not like it just because punk rock 'said so'. But also punk did clear out a lot of cobwebs. I grew up in the '70s but I didn't like the '70s (all those flares and stuff). Instead I use to watch old films with people like the Rat Pack and I liked their sharp suits, pointed shoes and smart hair.

I remember there was Russ (Wilkins) and me and a band called Gash in the Medway Towns. There wasn't many of us into punk rock. It wasn't like we could go down the pub with a dozen of our punk rock mates. But we did meet Billy (Childish) or as we knew him in those days, 'Steve the punk'. Then we formed the Pop Rivets after Russ and I went to see Gash playing. Gash inspired in a way where we thought we could do better (like you do when you're teenagers).

So, yeah, we got into going to see punk bands and in them days you go to London and on the same night you would have the Buzzcocks, Generation X or the Vibrators playing. My first Clash gig was on the Hastings Pier and they were playing with Richard Hell and the Voidoids. I got into all that American punk stuff at the same time as getting into The Clash.

I had actually met The Clash before I knew who they were. I had a mate from school who moved to London and I went up to stay with him. Whilst there he said to me, 'I'm going off to see my mates who are in a band, do you wanna come?' We went to some rehearsal place in Camden Town and there was also an office type area where the band were sitting all in their leather jackets and punky hair. I remember sitting there feeling slightly embarrassed because I was only one with longish hair and flared trousers. And I remember Strummer leaning back on a chair next to a pay phone. He was waiting to put a coin into the slot and had the phone receiver to his ear and when the time came he tried pushing the coin into the slot with his foot but it pinged out and flew off up into the air.

Apart from gigs the next time I bumped into Joe Strummer was when I was depping for a band called Ten Benson. We supported him for about five dates. I got him to sign my ride cymbal. He died soon after.

Bruce Brand.

RAVE

Raver Keith Davis remembers some classic moments.

I started off as a punk back in 79 aged 13 and was in a low level punk band who used to play local gigs (Slough) and various support slots in London. After a few years I was still listening to punk (still do) but I knew something was stirring and I knew that something huge was coming. I went to Ibiza in 1987 (by chance) and started hearing all of these new sounds in the clubs and the euphoria that was happening on the dance floors. I headed home to Slough after the holiday and knew this was going to be huge.

We started clubbing in London, going to anything from Northern Soul to disco nights. Then one night a friend of mine said, 'Come down to The Slough Centre with me'. As soon as I walked in I heard the strains of them sounds I had heard in Ibiza and I realised that the acid sound had reached the UK. As I walked in there was a huge wave of amazing sound, an incredible light show, lasers cutting through the smoke and people on dance platforms and rammed on the dance floor going crazy to this new sound. It was almost like I had found what I had been looking for all my life. Everyone was smiling and having the best time of their lives. That was the start of the first few years of the most hedonistic part of my life. Me and my mates would travel all around the M25 every weekend looking for the big ones, 20 or 30 thousand people was not uncommon. We carried on going to the Slough Centre, and clubs all over the place, Valbonnes in Maidenhead, Queens nightclub at the reservoir in Colnbrook and countless others. I eventually started putting on my own smaller scale events (Menace) and then opened up three record shops to get this music out there. I am now a 46 year old father of three, I feel blessed that I was the right age at the right time to be part of this thing. I can't personally see anything ever topping that scene or the joy it gave to thousands.

I had a Naf Naf brown suede bomber jacket that I used to wear out and about more during the week as it was too warm to wear out raving. I was the envy of loads of mates because it cost a fortune back then.

Keith Davis.

★ ★ ★

Steve Sparkes' account of Raving in the Summer of Love.

Sometime in about March or April 1989, three friends and I were keen to see what all the fuss was behind this acid house phenomenon that was sweeping the UK by storm.

Yes before you say it, 'Fucking 89? We were raving in the summer of love, 88!' I know there some of you out there that can lay claim to being one of the first 'cheesy quavers' on the planet, I've heard it all before, but for us four, this is our story.

The four of us being Ian, Richard, Steve (Richard's older brother) and myself. We were all down the pub, which an old school friend happened to live in, doing our usual thing playing pool, drinking Kronenburg 1664 and nipping out for the odd spliff now and then and listening to the *Deep Heat* album and Adamskis' *Liveanddirect* on the newly acquired CD juke box.

House music had been around a while and I myself can remember going to the Kent Hall discos on a Monday night (under 18s) and Saturday nights (over 18s) and listening to this new house sound, hearing the likes of Russ Brown's 'Find a Way', Raze's 'Jack the Groove' and Steve 'Silk' Hurley's 'Love Can't turn around' amongst others, thinking, *This has got something this, new sound*. So much better than the 'Shit factory' stuff that was also getting played at the time.

There was the four of us in the pub when a few of the others started to turn up, Mick and his ever trusty side kick Rusty, Daz, an old mate from the village I grew up in Jason, (lifelong friend to me) plus a few others. This was a Friday night and people were making plans for the weekend, bit of billy and an 'enry, sorted!

It wasn't long before discussions started to turn to this rave thing that was taking over a lot of people's weekends. There was talk of a Biology party taking place the next night at a secret location, all we had to do was get tickets and find out where the venue was and we were away.

Plans were made to meet up the next morning to get up to Oxford Street and Soho market to suss out this scene. So it was that I picked the other three up in my trusty, no rusty, old MG Metro and we set off up the M20 to London. All the way up there, with the tunes blaring, we were buzzing with the excitement of finding out what the shops and market had in stall for us, records, clothing, fliers and the chance of securing a ticket for the Biology rave happening (somewhere) that night.

On arrival in London we made straight for Soho and found somewhere to park, yes, you could quite easily back then. We had a mooch around Berwick Street Market and found our way to a [well-known] record store where Ian got a copy of the Frankie Knuckles album on the Trax label, a true classic which I'm also privileged to own.

While we were in there we enquired about the aforementioned Biology rave that night, the guy behind the counter was a bit cagey to start with but eventually sold us tickets for the sum of twenty quid each, bearing in mind this was 1989 and twenty quid was quite a bit then, but "fuck it" we all said, and bought the tickets. We all came out of that shop beaming from ear to ear at the thought of going to a proper rave and not the usual clubs in town or a house party or village hall disco.

Next we made our way to Mash clothing store, which was one of the reasons I wanted to go, eager to acquire some new clobber. Once finding the shop we had a good search through the stuff in there, taking the piss out of some of it shouting "Here moosh, who the fuck would wear this?" much to the annoyance of other shoppers and staff. While in there I bought myself what could only be likened to a hippie hoody, for want of a better description, I must've looked a right ★★★★ in it but at the time I felt like the 'mutt's nuts'.

After spending the day in London, we were buzzing back down the M20 to Maidstone and after dropping the lads off it was in, dinner, shower, change and back out again, round to Steve and Richard's house to meet up with Ian and get to the pub. We eventually set off back up the motorway, it was well into Saturday night by this time. The thing to do with these illegal parties was to tune into one of the pirate radio stations and listen out for meeting points, our choice being the great old station Sunrise, which everyone used to tape the sets being played by the then up-and-coming DJ's of the time, some of which went on to become household names, and play them back in their cars. This was quite difficult to do living at the bottom of the Downs and London being up over the other side, you either had to know someone who lived quite high up or drive around listening out for a good signal and try to tape it, something I used to do a bit later when I worked in a bakers as a night packer in Bermondsey and still have a friend's FM tape from Christmas 1990.

We eventually found out our first meeting point was Blackheath, actually on the heath, so after shooting about all over London we headed for there. Thinking back we must've really caned the petrol driving here, there and everywhere but we were still buzzing with the excitement and anticipation of getting to this Biology do, with our new clobber on and the distinctive 'diddly diddly diddly diddly' opening bars of Frankie Knuckles' 'Your Love,' a sound that still gives me tingles on the back of my neck and memories flooding back, it was like a 'pied piper' type sound calling all us teenagers to some far off field to trudge around in mud, off your face.

Once at Blackheath quite a few cars had started to gather and there was people standing on bonnets of cars dancing to car stereos pumping the acid beats, obviously on the gear already, we met up with a few like-minded people from different areas and all got chatting, the thrill of going raving in everyone's eyes. After a fair bit of socialising someone shouted to hush up a bit, they were going to give out the next meeting point. The word soon got around that it was to be in front of Charing Cross station on the Strand so into the cars we piled and shot up the A2 to central London where, again, quite a few cars had gathered and the people there looked like the real hardcore ravers who'd done this many times before, I can remember admiring these two dudes with their long, centre parted hair and almost hippy style clothing, thinking they looked cool.

After a bit more banter the next meeting point was announced over the radio, Liphook, fucking Liphook? Where the fuck is that? Turns out it's down the A3 in Hampshire, for fuck's sake! So in we get, find a petrol station, fill up and we're off across London to pick up the A3 and before long we're going past Tolworth

Towers and on our way, the novelty rapidly wearing off, well, for muggings here anyway, as I'd stayed sober as the designated driver. We finally get to Liphook, or the outskirts anyway, and by now quite a convoy of motors had built up and there we are, like the blind leading the blind, trying to find our final destination.

We ended up driving up and down country lanes looking for sign of lasers in the sky or the boom boom of the bass of a big open air party in a field, each time following a different car saying, "Here we go, these look like they know where they're going…" Fat fucking chance of that and couple with the growing interest of the local old bill and me panicking as I knew at least one person in the car was 'holding'. We ended up taking stock of the situation, franticly searching for a signal from the pirate station when all of a sudden it's announced it's not in poxy Liphook and we've got to get to South Mims Service Station as this is the next meeting point, I gotta tell you I was ready to say bollocks to it and piss off home there and then, but, being the driver and seeing the others wanting to get to this party I soldiered on so it was back up the A3 onto the M25 and off to South Mims.

When we got there this whole fiasco of a night seemed like it was all going to be worth it as the car park was packed with hundreds of ravers dancing on car bonnets and generally having a blinding Saturday night. Everyone was waiting for that radio message to let us know where this party was going to be but to be honest I was glad to be out of the driving seat for a bit and mill about South Mims Service Station chatting to people off their tits (and having a good gore at the copious amounts of fanny some of the geezers had in tow).

Time was getting on now and it must've been about 3AM when word started to get out that it had been given out on the radio that the Rave had indeed taken place in Liphook but had been shut down by the police.

We ended up getting back on the motorway and home in the early hours completely shattered but it never dampened our spirits as the next day we all had a good laugh about 'what could've been'. We ended up going to copious amounts of raves together in the end and had a fucking good few years at it going to parties all over the place and some right seedy ones at that, not to mention some right dodgy East London clubs and warehouse parties and nearly every time someone had their car stereo nicked but I could be here all day reminiscing and I'm sure you've all got your own memories and stories to tell but to me raving was a great time to while away my late teens and early twenties.

Steve Sparkes.

★ ★ ★

A dance music account from the '90s by Spencer Vinten

After the Indie and Madchester scene fizzled out, I was propelled into the Rave scene on the back of a random invite to a house party in Camden in late 89. It was twenty quid to get in but with entry came a free Love Dove. Little did I know how much that one pill was going to change my life. This party had no dress code and absolutely no attitude, just a very pleasant young man (who turned out to be an old school friend) with a wide smile who greeted us at the door. Once inside the lights were dim. There was very little furniture and in the kitchen three fridges full of bottled water only.

The music was a blend of warm, smooth house music. There were DJs upstairs and downstairs which was totally new to me at the time. Each track melted seamlessly into the next, creating a constant mix of wonderful melodic rhythms. It was impossible not to dance to it. 'Izit-Stories (the Jackanory mix)' is the tune, with its vocal loop, that just says it all about the night.

One of the big things I remember is the overall lovely vibe and the fact that it didn't matter whose eyes you met with or person you spoke to, it was always met with a warm smile and a pleasant response. Conversations flowed and new friends were easily made. I left there feeling like I had not only found the latest new thing but I had seen the light, I had awoken, been re-born and an excitement that I had never felt before had risen within me. From then on it was always about getting into parties anywhere near or far, legal or illegal and later on large Raves like Raindance and Reincarnation and many others.

The music was infectious and hypnotic. The party goers were all like-minded and non-judgemental. Sound people with the sole intention to have fun. There was no racism, no class divides, all were equal and were there to party and smile in a driven hedonistic musical heaven. We lived for the weekend, the latest tune, a disused warehouse party, M25 convoys looking for Raves. It was a life-changing scene. View points shifted. Ideals were forgotten. Compliance was not an option. It was all for one and one for all.

Tunes that mark those days for, me are Moby 'Go (the Woodstick Mix)', Orbital's 'Chime' and Gat Décor's 'Passion'. I was soon DJing myself and throwing small local parties to spread the word, the love and the fabulous music. The Rave scene in my opinion changed the way of the world or definitely in the UK for good. It is now firmly placed in mainstream music and the staple diet for many party people, young or old, with so many variations and reflections of the original scene.

Long may it continue. Love and Peace.

Spencer Vinten.

★ ★ ★

Snowy with a 1989 account of a typical night trying to get to a Rave.

The police officer went on to describe the carnage left behind by the ravers and the invasion of people's good night's sleep. He also mentioned the impact on wildlife; the new drug E's sweeping through every town, hamlet and city in the United Kingdom called Ecstasy. More footage of raves showed wide-eyed young people bopping to the trance like music in dry-ice filled venues whilst impressive visuals splashed their lights across them. Everything about the images felt familiar to me and I congratulated myself on being a successful raver who also contributed to the second 'Summer of Love'.

Typically for the summer of 1989 I would put my favourite baseball cap onto my head and pull the pony tail through it. And then put on my Timberlands boots... the best boots ever made and perfect for dancing in fields and warehouses, then grab some money (twenty for entrance to a rave and twenty for something else) and raced down stairs, through the front room and out of the front door, yelling back, 'See you later'. Then I would be on my way to meet my mates.

Craig's white Vauxhall would be parked alongside Steve's red Metro and more cars would be parked besides. The doors on Craig's car would be wide open and he would be playing something like 'Ride on Time' or 'Rhythm Is Rhythm'. Craig would be wearing his new Mash clobber and purple desert boots. Steve was also wearing desert boots in a pastel pale green. He would also wear his bright red long-sleeve shirt with golden shapes and patterns on it.

We would probably discuss Pete's crazy leg dancing at the Red Lion in Gravesend and take the piss out of him for a bit, before moving on to somebody else. Craig would turn the volume up further on his car stereo so we could listen to the announcements on Centre Force 88.3. The Deejays would be suggesting a rave was going to happen somewhere in the Essex countryside. That was the place to be on this Saturday night. What we would wait for was the addresses of meeting points. Rumours would have been circulating all week about a rave somewhere but even an hour or so before we would sometimes not know.

There was more laughter and sorting out arrangements and then the Deejay would reveal that the first meeting point of the night was going to be on Blackheath. Craig would announce it was time to be heading off and the crowd of boys would disperse into various cars. Craig would lead the convoy of adventurers out of the car park up the hill and onto the M20. Seven car-loads of ravers in all, charging down the motorway in the direction of the meeting point on Blackheath common. The buzz and adrenalin kicking in.

Each of the seven cars would be tuned into Centre Force radio. The night would promise something special and all would be totally on board. The Centre Force Dee jay would inform its listeners that Guru Josh or Adamski or a load of other deejays were going to be at the rave.

The word is there's a meeting point on Blackheath common so we head there. About three miles before we reached Blackheath, the Centre Force Deejay announced that there was going to be another meeting point at a hotel on the A2. Craig changes direction and the six cars behind him followed. Within five minutes of driving at eighty miles an hour, Craig steers his car into the hotel car park.

There's a few more cars already there that appear to have ravers in them. Everybody eyes one another up suspiciously. The other six cars soon follow and park awkwardly around the car park. Steve pulls up beside Craig's car and winds down his window. Steve is about to yell something when I notice the smile on his face suddenly disappear. Three police cars screeched into the car park and one stops in the entrance way therefore blocking the cars' exits. The police cars surrounded the cars full of ravers and coppers jump out of their cars and instructed all the drivers to switch off their engines. Craig twists the tuner on the radio to disguise that he had been listening to Centre Force.

'Bollocks,' says Craig, 'They must have intercepted the info about the meeting points'.

'Yes, this could mean an early night for us all,' I reply.

'Yea, trust us to be the first ones here. If we had not of driven so fast we could of spotted the old Bill from the A2' added another mate.

'Can you all step out of the car please, lads?' says the booming voice of an older police officer.

Everyone then gets slowly out of the car. The police officer asked them to step a few feet away from the car. Police officers dive into the cars, giving them a thorough search for drugs. One officer pushed and heaved the back seat in Craig's car until he hands out the entire seat. Craig looks like he is going to cry.

'So where are you lads off to tonight?' asked the copper.

'Just driving around,' Craig mumbles.

'Just driving around, eh?! I don't believe you. I think you have your sights set on going to one of those illegal raves'.

'Not us,' says Pete, gurning.

'You look like ravers to me,' says the copper. The copper then nods towards the other cars in the car park and adds, 'Your mates look like ravers too'.

There's some more banging and clattering as the police officer inside Craig's car does his best to dismantle the interior. We all keep quiet and try to look innocent. Another much younger policeman worked his way around each raver and asked them to remove all the items in their pockets. I grin at the sight of lighters, Rizlas, tissues, hankychiefs and chewing gum wrappers. The whole debacle lasts about thirty minutes and then the old police officer in charge of the operation announces that everything was ok but advised that we all turn around and drive back down the M20. We have no intention of doing so but agreed just so that we can shake off the Plod and make a quick get-away to Blackheath before everyone else moves on to the next meeting point.

The coppers jump back into their cars with disappointed faces and drive off. Craig suggests that we wait five minutes before we set off again for Blackheath. We all laugh and joke about their encounter with the rave busters. In the meantime Craig tunes in again to Centre Force and the Deejay is still instructing everybody to go to Blackheath. The Deejay even announced that he had heard that a bust had recently occurred at the hotel. We feel like heroes.

Once Craig is satisfied that the coast is clear, he leads the charge again out of the car park and down the A2 towards Blackheath. As soon as we have exited the A2, the traffic slows due to the volume of cars heading in the direction of the common. It took a further ten minutes to reach Blackheath. Everyone in the car is astounded by the sheer volume of cars parked all over the common. I estimated that there must have been five hundred cars scattered on the grassy heath. This is one fucking big meeting point.

Craig's mounted the curb and skidded towards a space not far from a small roundabout. The rest of our convoy followed suit and we park in a circle. I've jumped out of the car first and the site of the hundreds of ravers eager to get raving excites me. We have been at meeting points before but we have never witnessed anything like this before. It feels great to be a part of it. Police cars are parked on the fringes of the heath and the coppers roam in amongst the raver's cars wearing their fluorescent overcoats. They glow in the parked cars headlights. Car after car has its doors wide open and belt out music from the various pirate radio stations. We even spot a few kids dancing on the roofs of their cars. The site is spectacular.

Craig and I snake our way in and out of the cars, occasionally chatting to other ravers. The atmosphere is one of anticipation, friendliness and nervous excitement. There are several older males holding brick-size mobile phones to their ears. They are part of the organisers of the rave. They are surrounded by ravers asking questions and waiting for information regards the location of the next meeting point or the pot of the Gold itself.

'E's, E's' whispers the voice of a young man dressed in yellow dungarees and wearing a red beret on his head. The man weaves his way in and around the waiting ravers. A few seconds later I hear another voice advertising purple ohms and black microdots. I look up into the black, star-lit London sky. It looks still and distant and a universe away from the chaos below on the heath. I knew that this is going to be one of the best nights of my life.

There appears to be some instructions about another meeting point from the men with their mobile phones. Ravers started to jump into the cars and dart this way and that attempting to find and follow the leader. Craig and I race back to our vehicle and jump inside. Like a well-drilled military operation, all the ravers returned to the cars with haste and joined the massive convoy. The police do their best to ascertain what's happening and keep up but they cannot.

'What's the word?' I ask.

'The word is there is another meeting point at the South Ockendon service station'.

'Where the fuck is that?' moans Pete.

'It's off the M25 in Essex', Craig informs him before skidding off the grassy common and hitting the tarmac at speed. There's a whoosh of excitement in the car as we follow a green Golf GTE in front. Craig turns up the volume on the radio and 808 State rocks the inside of the car.

We drive back down the A20 alongside other cars evidently full of ravers. We merged with the M25 and hurtled down it towards the Dartford tunnel. As we approach the tunnel we notice that the police have closed several of the gates in an attempt to prevent the cars full of ravers crossing the Thames and entering Essex and finding their way to the rave. Fortunately Craig swung the car away from the closed gates and they managed to sneak through undetected. We bolt through the tunnel along with other successful cars of ravers. As we exit the tunnel, we feel confident that we are going to reach the rave intact. I'm not familiar with the area of Essex but trust that Craig would find the service station.

On our arrival at the South Ockendon service station, we could already see that several cars were leaving. Craig pulls into the service station because he also needed to refuel. It was apparent that we have lost three of our convoy. Craig fills his car with petrol and chats with the ravers in the car behind who were also filling up with fuel. They informed him that they were from Hertfordshire and that the rave was nearby. Craig relays the information about the location of the rave to us.

Craig has arranged to follow the ravers from Hertfordshire and we set off down the A13. As we left the service station more and more cars of ravers pulled into it. We get the sense that this rave is going to be a massive affair. Craig follows the car in front and Steve follows close on the heels of his bumper behind. We drive through Thurrock and North Stifford until we reach a small village called Orsett. There is a stunned silence inside the car. The adrenalin inside us is buzzing. We sense the rave is nearby. The hypnotic sounds of 'Sueno Latino' on Centre Force reflect our mood and expectations.

We drive through country lanes which were filled with parked cars. Police officers in the fluorescent coats glowed as they lined up along a stretch of lane that led to the rave. They remind me of the lights on the runways in airports. The police had given up trying to deter the cars full of ravers. They had no choice as twenty thousand excited and determined youths caused havoc.

The car in front finds a spot big enough to park in and as our car passes them they shouted out, 'Have a good one'. We can hear the thumbing deep bass of the house music in the distance. We can see Steve in his Metro behind us bouncing around inside as he responds to the music coming from the rave.

Craig finds the car space and chooses a spot. We gather our coats and jackets and jumped excitedly out of the car. There's a group of men twenty yards in front of them clutching their mobile phones and waving to us to hurry up.

'Well then,' I say, 'Nice one for getting us here, Craig.'

'Piece of piss mate,' he replies.

'So what do you think, twenty quid to get in?'

'Maybe twenty five, but look at the size of the rave. It's massive, our biggest yet'.

I soak in the sights and sounds of the rave as we walk nearer to it. We can spot a Ferris wheel and other fairground rides. There are flashing laser lights and psychedelic images being projected all over the site of the rave. We prepare ourselves for the next seven hours of dancing and look forward to the sun coming up at five when the Deejays will respond to it by playing The Beloved's 'The Sun Rising'.

Snowy.

SCOOTER BOYS

Scootering *magazine journalist*
Mark Sargeant tells a story.

Looking back at my formative years when I was a teenager is unnerving, some of the things that were 'normal'. Discovering girls, clothes, beer, fags football and music all within a few months of each other. Ok, football-wise I'd been indoctrinated into supporting my local team, Oxford United, from almost the off by my dad, as I became a teenager, I'd go with other lads and get involved in both home and, more so, away day excursions. Adopted or tolerated by the local skinheads and suedeheads who had at least 3 years on me, I learnt to ride scooters, Lambrettas, and would bunk off school on Wednesdays to 'work' on a market stall. Not just any market stall, this one offered Levi's jeans and Sta-Prest, Ben Sherman, Brutus and Jaytex button-down collar shirts as well as Harrington jackets and Crombie-style coats. A handy way of earning a few quid as well as getting a huge discount on all the clobber on offer. Eventually my school had enough of my antics, which resulted in expulsion a few months before I was 14.

As for the music, in the very early '70s it was Trojan Reggae, Stax, Atlantic and Tamla Motown. There was a youth club in Oxford City centre, The Catacombs. It was there that I made my debut as a DJ, for me the soul sides just shaded it, especially as it was soul that the girls seemed to prefer.

Early 1972 I had my first encounter with what would become known as Northern Soul, a car full of us had been to an away match in the Midlands, and on the way back, at the suggestion/insistence of Coco (a Suedehead from Bicester who went to the The Golden Torch), we stopped off in Wolverhampton at a place called The Catacombs. I'd have been 14 at the time, I was full of alcohol and pharmaceuticals, and can't remember much about that particular experience, apart from it was hot, dark and the music seemed to be absolutely brilliant. Mind you I was trying out all my best chat up lines, which for once failed every time.

Saturday nights, football away days excepted, were often spent at Dunstable's California Ballrooms. Bit of a trek from Oxford, but even with a midnight finish, most nights at the Cali' were excellent. There was always a live act in the main room, invariably an American Soul outfit or act, I saw Arthur Connelly, Ben E King, KC and The Sunshine Band, George and Gwen McRae, The first 'Philly Busters ' tour package, Edwin Starr, The Four Tops, The Temptations and many more. Downstairs was The Devil's Den, where resident DJ Brother Louie served up the hottest new import 45s. Working in what, for a short time, was Oxford's cutting edge menswear outlet, Stag Shop; every day the music on the in-house 8-track was Soul. Baggies, both pleated and high waisted as well as bowling shirts, leather bomber jackets and 3/4 length coats were first available off the shelf from there. I'd occasionally browse through the assistant manager's copy of *Blues and Soul* magazine, when *Black Music* magazine came out he'd buy that too. Tony Cumming's first Northern Soul special, starting off with Eddie Foster's spirit visiting the underground UK scene, had quite an appeal. Russell Acott's, a music shop that stocked a massive amount of soul music in the upstairs record emporium, both old and brand new imports, proved to be very helpful. In the *Black Music* magazine feature was a 'playlist' from the scene's past. The Northern Soul scene sounded interesting, naively I tentatively enquired if any of the records were still available. On British release, from stock, among my acquisitions were: Bobby Sheen's 'Dr. Love', the Poets' 'She Blew a Good Thing', Bobby Hebb's 'Love, Love, Love'.

Fellow Oxford United supporter, Graham Hilsdon, dropped into Stag Shop late September 1973, there was a coach trip to Wigan Casino arranged for early October, was I interested? You bet I was, via working in the shop I spread the word, and all the seats were snapped up rather quickly. Membership arrived, a blue one, which I still have today, it was a few weeks after the Casino's first anniversary that I made my first trip to an all-nighter. A defining night in my life, as once I took my first look off the balcony at the packed dance floor below, I was hooked. Even though the windscreen on the coach shattered on the way back to Oxford, I wasn't put off. Clichéd though it may be, my first visit to the Casino was a life-shaping moment.

Excursions to the Casino were every four to six weeks, some of my earliest original 45 purchases included Gwen and Ray's 'Build Your House (On A Strong Foundation)', Christine Cooper's 'Heartaches Away My Boy' and Williams and Watson's 'Too Late'. Visits to Russell Acott turned up lots of gems, a chap called Brian who worked there on Saturdays had been buying Tamla Motown for years, which led to some nice UK items joining my collection. Cream of which was Kim Weston's 'I'm Still Loving You', Tamla Motown TMG 511 white demo, for a large brandy!

I'd changed jobs, by now I was working as Bar Manager in Oxford's then top nightclub, Scamps, – classic uptown, late night, meat market part of the Star group who had a whole complex of premises close to Blackpool's North Pier, as well as a chain of clubs across the UK. Work commitments, as in 2.30-3am finish 6 nights a week didn't allow more than one monthly night off required to travel north for the 3 hours to the Casino. Train, hitching, the Portsmouth coach, minibus trips, car convoys, got to the Casino many different ways. John 'Kojak' Harvey with his Inter City Soul Club, a kind a travelling soul road show, was quite active at the time, blagged myself a DJ slot at the Oxford all-dayers, which were invariably on a Sunday, ICSC also started holding all-nighters in Yate near Bristol. A 50-mile drive. I attended most of the Yate niters, under Kojak, then Dinks under the Southern Soul Club banner, and finally Mick MacAvoy, who post-Yate held several niters at a hotel in Swanage. Yate nights lights would go on in Scamps, and from seemingly nowhere a horde of people in wide trousers (or flared skirts females, most of the time!) eyes as wide as their strides & chewing gum frantically, invaded. Collecting, washing and restocking the bar, while I cashed up the last till. Off to Yate within 10 minutes, driven down by the then-Scamps resident DJ Nigel, who had a Transit with benches, fitted each side.

Also during the Yate era, I went to most of the Bisley Pavilion all-nighters, while in Abingdon, the Youth centre wanted to raise funds for all weather 5–a side footy pitches. They oversaw monthly all-nighters, and occasional all-dayers. Towards the end of the two years or so there were a few funk/jazz funk all-dayers too. As well as Northern Soul, I was also into the funk and (soul inclined) disco tunes too. Very occasionally taking a trip to the Lacy Lady, The Goldmine, and later the Rio Didcot, where I guested as warm-up DJ a few times. Saturday lunchtime session at Scamps, Oxford was 100% new imports and promo only British (pre-) releases that was my baby for the few years it ran, people coming in from a 30-40 mile radius of Oxford every week. Mind you, at that time Oxford had some excellent clothes shops as well as Russell Acott, who had the latest US imports arrive every Saturday morning. The Jazz Funk all-dayers in Reading (I guested at the one where the Jazz-Funk room & Northern Soul room changed rooms, Jazz Funk in the main room for the first time.

At the previous Reading all-dayer, Chris Hill led a conga into the main room & put Magic Fly on the decks; Cockney Mick took it off and snapped the 12" in half! Purley, Alexander Palace, the first Caister, Southgate Royalty were all happenings I went to, plus DJing on Sunday nights in the New Inn Cowley Road, Oxford.

During the golden era, I only made it to Blackpool Mecca a handful of times, Cleethorpes Pier and St Ives were others I visited even less. Abingdon all-nighters (although the venue was strange, some christened it the goldfish bowl) saw plenty of rare originals change hands there for very pocket friendly amounts. Wigan never disappointed, Bisley was always fun, and Yate was excellent. The card schools & backgammon as the sun filtered through the curtains to a backdrop (!) of top quality rare soul, I'd go as far as to say that Yate at its peak laid down the blueprint for the Stafford style of sounds. After I had changed jobs from working at Scamps, a typical Yate excursion went something like this: meet up in Abingdon, several cars would head off together to Newbury, descending on a pub called the Anchor, (or the Ship), which the local soul fraternity had stocked the jukebox with Northern Soul 'reissues'. When Yate was on, it was a magnet to most travelling west; then, en masse we'd head off towards Yate, pausing for a while at Leigh Delamere services, meeting others Yate bound.

1978 I acquired a Lambretta GP125, within 12months there was a sizeable number travelling by scooter to the early 6T's rhythm 'n' soul nites as well as early RSG bashs in Hemel Hempstead. All-nighter wise over the next few years, Peterborough, Stafford, Chesterfield, 100 Club, Leighton Buzzard and later Bradford Queen's Hall. I was getting regular DJ work at the RSG & Bradford niters as well as guest spots elsewhere.

Workwise, I had gone back to electrical engineering, a 5-day week, 39 then 37 hours, freed up more leisure time. As well as regularly going to rare soul happenings, I was also doing the national scooter rallies, competing in scooter sport events, as well as during 9 months of the year still going to most of Oxford United's games. Wembley 86 was the pinnacle of the Yellows' achievements, in the then old first division and league cup winners (now it's Oxford's 2nd season outside of the football league).

Although I'd always swapped and sold 45s, it was during the '80s that, like many other soulies, I pruned many classic, '60s style Northern Soul discs from my collection. Having a cosmopolitan taste in soul, many went in swaps for, or to fund the purchase of rare '70s and '80s items. Canal Tavern was a superb soul night with Rod Dearlove at the helm, a real collector's soulmine too, the quality of music played there was ultra-high.

I'd been asked to contribute to a brand new scooter magazine, *British Scooter Scene*, which became *Scooter Scene*, then eventually merged with *Scootering*. Marriage broke up; I was freelancing for the local paper as well as one or two other publications, so I took redundancy from the factory. Venues such as the Hacienda, Manchester & the Ministry of Sound were visited a few times after I'd been to a few early raves, similar to the rare soul scene, but when you've found your own brand of champagne, others may be similar without actually pressing all your buttons, I found. Bizarrely I ended up promoting live music, with work commitments, the soul end of things went on the back-burner for a few years, only getting to functions on odd occasions. Although, one of the venues I worked for via my suggestion introduced a night named 'Retro', format being classic soul & funk from the '60s to mid-80s, which proved to be unbelievably popular. Gave me a smug satisfaction introducing tunes like Carol Anderson's 'Sad Girl', James Fountain's 'Seven Day Lover', Glenda McCleod's 'No Stranger to Love' to a whole new audience.

Once you get bitten by the rare soul bug, you stay infected, and there is no cure, Metropolitan Soul Club started to hold all-nighters at The Rocket in North London, excellent venue, some superb obscurities, shame about the northern scene's politics!

I DJed at a couple of the warm-up sessions across Holloway Road, and had a guest spot (both main room and Modern room) at one of the niters. Also I guested at Togetherness weekender in Fleetwood, nr. Blackpool. Since around that time I have been buying, selling and trading rare soul records. There's still a handful I'm looking for, IF the price or deal is right. In recent years I've guested at Bisley, both main and modern rooms as well as Talk of the South, RSG and Aylesbury soul club nights. Over the years I've amassed over 10,000 45s, and 12,000 12" and albums on vinyl, not to mention CDs, the vast majority of which are soul records. Even now I can't resist ferreting through second-hand vinyl wherever I encounter any! Still collecting, still enjoying (in the main) and still, when I can, getting to various soul nights and niters, more years later than I prefer to admit to.

Mark Sargeant.

★ ★ ★

Scootering Paul Crittenden On Dr. Martens.

Finally starting to lose my puppy fat at the grand old age of 14 was a big turning point in my life. A few years of being taunted for being overweight had left a lasting impression on my life! I was still heavy but adulthood had crept up on me and my stature meant I started to gain a new found confidence I'd not had before! Finding music and fashion changed my direction. Wanting to belong and accepted by my peers was high on my agenda. I lived on a council estate in Maidstone which had a reputation not really deserved. Surrounded by a mixture of punks, mods, skinheads, soul boys and hippies I found myself drawn to being part of a group. I chose Skinhead; cropped hair, Ben Shermans, Fred Perrys, boots and braces were top of my shopping list. Convincing my parents was another matter so with a need for my own money I started a paper round to fund my thirst for fashion and music. After a few months of saving I finally found myself in Baileys Shoe Shop at the top of Maidstone High Street trying on a pair of cherry red 8 hole Dr. Martens boots. Clutching the box under my arm I quickly walked home grinning from ear to ear at my new purchase. The smell of new leather filled the air as I stood in my bedroom admiring myself in the mirror feeling very proud of myself. I finally felt I belonged to something and my first venture into town to show off my new boots changed me. No longer the long-haired fat kid I now gained respect in a funny sort of way. I noticed old people cross the road rather than walk past me and no one wanted to make eye contact. Such is the kudos of being a skin. An instant friend base of like-minded people dossing around in Benchley gardens, drinking the odd bottle of Merrydown, jumping trains, fighting and glue sniffing. Coupled with my haircut, and clothes, my boots were my badge, my pride, my distinction from the other kids in my school. No matter what I wore, even in school uniform, the boots made me feel something. If I'd of shown the same attention to polishing my boots as I did my school work I would of come out of school with straight A's. I didn't care about school, as I lived for the school bell and the time I could start my stroll into town to meet my mates. A 2 week school trip planned to Spain meant packing my boots in my luggage and a knowing smile that I could wear civvies for a while. Whilst everyone was sitting on the beach in their swimming costumes, I was sat in my full skinhead regalia with my DM's shining in the sun. Madness if I think about it now, in ninety degree heat. My chosen footwear stayed with me until I was seventeen when the need to get mobile meant a change in direction. The second wave of mods gave way to the scooter boy and I was instantly drawn to scooters and their roots. Skinheads had come from mod beginnings and the clothes and attitudes were very similar. Scooter boy encompassed all fashions from skinhead to psychobilly all drawn together with a passion for everything Lambretta and Vespa. My DM's again became an integral part of the look but with a safety side when riding. They looked better with age and every knock, scratch and crease told a story, the soles barely worn which considering I'd worn them for 3 years seemed incredible. Now, the worse side of middle age, I still have a pair of cherry reds in the cupboard, as I have had since I was fourteen. Still cherished, still polished, a sign of my youth I won't give up! To quote Alexei Sayle, 'It's not class or ideology, class, creed or roots, the only thing that unites us is Dr. Martens boots.'

Paul Crittenden.

* * *

Gareth Brown, extracted from his classic book, Scooter Boys.

By the end of 1980, the scooter-riding Mod revivalist was well established, and like his ancestors, had a particularly healthy fashion scene. New styles would (as they had in the '60s) come and go week by week, and sometimes day by day. This aspect of Modernism was slightly lost in later years, as uniformity crept in, standardising styles and making obsolete the innovative 'Face'.

I can still vividly recall visiting Barrons, a puritan '60s night club in Leigh-on-Sea, near Southend in Essex. You were expected to turn up on your suitably trimmed scooter (in my case a 1962 Vespa Sportique) at least half an hour before the doors opened and strut around the car park with your parka removed (so long as it wasn't raining) like a model on a cat walk. You would allow yourself and your scooter to be scrutinized, while tentatively studying others. This wasn't done clinically, as you would talk, laugh and chat amongst your fellow Mods, but all the time you'd be clocking what's what! Parallel pastel hipsters, suede brogues and tight turtle neck sweaters could be in one week – then cords, bowling shoes and cycling shirts the next.

The only thing you could really be sure of were suede and leather box jackets, as these cost so much they were always acceptable. You didn't have time to get bored. The constant rejuvenation of image left you in a swirl. It was exciting, exhilarating and extremely expensive but I and many others loved it. If you couldn't keep up, you had to keep out. Unfortunately, it was this last train of thought that was to bring about this wave's downfall. Elitism became rife, alienating many whose hearts were in the right place. It was the prolonged paisley-peace period of mid-81 before most people managed to catch up, but by then it was too late. There was a need for something new!

By the Christmas 1981 there appeared to be three separate camps emerging from the mainstream of Mod. These became more apparent in the first months of 1982. Those motivated wholly by the ever-changing image had moved on via natural transgression to the next fashionable phase after paisley: Psychedelia. Closely resembling the trendy dandies from whom the Hippie boom had taken off at the end of the '60s, this faction soon went their own separate way, and in time fizzled out. A cultural back-lash caused many to return to the more traditional image of Modernism through the re-introduction of suits, While the third main group seemed to settle for a more contemporary and casual style of dress as they gravitated closer to the scooter. With their walking-out wardrobe centred virtually entirely around jeans, denim jackets, olive green American MA1 bomber jackets (which soon gained the nick-name of scooter jackets) and an assortment of footwear such as base-ball, Boxing, Monkey and later Dr. Martens boots. They could still be seen as part of the Mod movement, although starting to follow a different path.

Gareth Brown.

ROCKERS

Brian, memories of a Rocker.

I got there first, on my Triumph T120, because as the organiser, it was expected of me to do so. Once parked up, I lit a Guards cigarette, and started my wait. Frank arrived next and nicked a fag from me (his usual M.O.), and so it began. We had arranged to meet on the forecourt of a pub (forget the name of the pub, now), which was situated by the Tee Junction of the Stockport and Wilmslow road, in Macclesfield, Cheshire (within a decade, these forecourts, by necessity, would became re-classified as pub car parks). Those we were waiting for were coming from Buxton, Leek, Macclesfield, Stockport, Stoke, Stockport, Alderly Edge, and even a few from Matlock Bath (which in later years became something of a Biker, and Bike event, staging point),.

Because there were far fewer vehicles on the roads back then (1965), coupled with the fact that it was 8am Easter Bank Holiday Monday morning, the only vehicles that Frank and I could see, and the only vehicles we could hear, were the tuned Triumphs, BSAs, and Norton motorcycles that were thundering towards us, in dribs and drabs, out of the day's drizzle.

As each fresh arrival pulled up, the volume and intensity of the chatter, the banter, and the rev-rev-revving of engines from those who did not switch off, grew. It really was very exciting. Most of us were still in our early twenties, and all of us were fully pumped with anticipation and exhilaration.

Every second seemed to see a further two or three arrive to swell our ranks, and every second saw the curtains on the upstairs windows of the pub twitch and flicker, as the confused and possibly concerned publican and his family tried to fathom out what was going on.

By 8.30am, the forecourt and adjoining pavements and pathways were packed with parked motorcycles. The drizzle gave way to sunshine, and as far as you could see, the water drips draped across the acres of chromed headlights and handlebars glistened like so many diamonds.

By 8.45am the publican, possibly fearing pillage and anarchy, had had enough, and called the Cavalry, who arrived at 8.55am in the form of a rather chubby, yet incredibly tough looking, flat-cap wearing policeman, who along with a slightly more slender, yet equally tough looking policeman, pulled up opposite us in a pale cream coloured Morris 1000, which had the word POLICE sign written in royal blue on each door...

I wandered over to meet the two officers with my mate Frank. I explained we were all meeting to go on a ride to Blackpool for the day, and added cheekily did they want to come with us, too? The chubbier of the two policemen said, "No, thank you," and "Hadn't you all best be on your way, then?" to which we agreed, so returned to the ranks, and barked out to all to mount their steed, and in a truly inspiring thunderous crescendo of blue smoke and speed, we hurtled off en-mass towards Wilmslow so as to circumnavigate our way through to the A6, and the start of our 80-mile jaunt to the Vegas of the North.

Brian.

★ ★ ★

Charlie – A Rocker who didn't like Mods.

I hated MODS. My mates hated MODS, and everyone we knew whose opinion mattered to us hated MODS. We had grown up in a world where men were men. My mates and I had all done two years in the Army (National Service), and so back in 1963, we viewed MOD as travesties! To us, the MOD girls looked and dressed like boys, the MOD boys looked and dressed like girls, and as for the abominations they rode, we just couldn't get our heads around why any teenager back then would choose to ride anything as slow and as un-gamely as a top-heavy scooter?

One of our gang (we called ourselves the 'Road Rockers' and had the same written on the backs of our leather bike jackets, one word on top of the other, in a design crafted from red painted letters edged with dozens and dozens of chrome studs), once suggested that maybe the MODS rode scooters to cure the insomnia that all the MODS down our way seemed to suffer from, as a result of continually taking the Purple Heart Uppers they that they seemed to be always scoffing like Smarties? We laughed for hours over this (and even as I sit here in 2015 as an old man, I still find that funny today:-D).

Our favourite place to go at the weekend was The Ace Café on the A1 in North London. This was a fantastic meeting place, had a great juke box, and even threw together a passable plate of egg and chips (burgers were almost unheard of back then), which we would wash down with gallons of strong tea. The Ace was also a great place to pick up chicks, as lots of young ladies who loved bikes would travel there by bus just to be seen by the boys on bikes who gathered there and, believe me, they were.

Sometimes blokes would come by bus, too. If these were known faces who did so because their bikes had bust, that was fine, and although we would take the mickey out of them mercilessly for being pedestrians (but we also made a point never to go too far, here, as we were all acutely aware that given the precarious home-tunes that most of our bikes had endured to varying degrees of competency, most of us were only a rev too hard away from suffering the same social indignity of a broken bike, at some point in the future, too), these lads were welcomed with open arms.

The male mugs who turned up by bus all dressed in leathers and carrying crash helmets who had obviously never owned – let alone ridden – a bike though (and believe me, there were a fair few of these idiots), once sussed, received a far different welcome, and quite often, a series of slaps if they ever over-stepped the mark, too.

We would normally arrive at The Ace early evening around 6pm, and once we'd had a Woodbine and some scoff, we would set about talking to the other Rockers arriving from other areas of London. Yes, we did all call ourselves Rockers. After all, that is what we were. We would look at each others race-replica bikes (even though sometimes such race-tunes were only cosmetic through the addition of Ace race bars and the removal of exhaust baffles so as to make an engine make the right noise), and swap notes and stories. Over time almost all the regulars got to know all the other Saturday night regulars. I suppose we did become a bit of a clique, but we would always welcome a new set of faces if their clobber and bikes where up to muster.

If it was cold or wet outside, most of the interactions with the girls would take place inside The Ace, where the booming beat of the Rock-n-Roll (strictly Rock-n-Roll you understand) records from the well-primed juke box made a brilliant back drop. Some of the girls would dance, but seldom would the blokes, as unless they'd brought a change of footwear with them, doing so in bike boots made them look like they lacked any form of co-ordination, which for those of us without a close lady friend, and who wanted one, that was not a good place to start.

Usually about 8pm people would start to drift off to other places, like other cafes a ride away, at the same sort of time that riders from other cafes would turn up at the Ace to replace them. This sort of bike and bike rider osmosis meant that although The Ace seemed packed with Rockers and bikes from tea time through to closing, seldom would the faces swelling those in attendance be the same at the end of the session as at the start. I LOVED this aspect of being a Rocker, especially as if we were lucky enough to attract the attention of one of the girls who showed up, providing she wasn't already attached (coz that'd cause the most ugly of kick-offs if she was), you could take her out for a breath-taking ride to impress her as you sped from café to café and venue to venue, and hopefully start a little romantic connection?

Believe it or not, apart from when we went to specific Rock and Roll Hops (you would now call them discos, I suppose), which were usually held in pub or club halls, we wouldn't actually drink much alcohol, but when we did go to a Hop, we would usually leave our bikes at home, wear our winkle-picker boots instead of our bike boots (so we could have a bit of a Bop if we wanted to), and drink until we properly had our fill (our usual poison would be a pint of mild, or a 50:50 mix of mild and bitter called a split, but never EVER the new fangled Lager drinks that were creeping in, as to us, these Lagers were purely the preserve of the fluffy idealistic Beat-Nicks and the girly male MODS, and not us real men). These were happy days.

Charlie.

SKINHEAD

A first generation skinhead, Nigel Harris.

First year of secondary school (Year Seven in modern speak) 1969 there was no other fashion, alright you had your Grebos (Rockers) and your Wallies (Hippies) but they were very much in the minority, your 'High Street Fashion' catered for us! Frank Wright Loafers, Silver Stud Brogues from Featherstone's or Pyes in Rochester, Ben Sherman and Brutus slim fit Shirts, Levi's Sta-Prest, Tonics from Silvers in Chatham (they had a closing down sale that must of gone on for about 20 years) and we had Rochester Market, where we bought our Harrington jackets. Burke and Hare was an unknown or long forgotten label that used to produce some lovely quality gear on the markets… Dog tooth check, Prince of Wales check, Tonic, trousers and suits, then we had the Guards Factory in Strood that made Crombie's, cheap enough especially if you knew someone who could get one out the back door!

My first pair of boots came courtesy of my dad, his old work boots, Doc Martens Astronauts, well they were once I'd cleaned them off chipped off all the cement and concrete and diligently sat there polishing them till I could see my face in them, slightly too big but this was sorted out by stuffing the toes with bog roll! Levi's or Lee jeans (Tesco's had just opened up in Chatham and my mum kindly bought me a pair of Delamare jeans, I was devastated, I never wore 'em!) rolled up just enough so that when you walked you flashed just a half inch of bright red towelling sock or some such other bright primary colour!

Shirts, quite a controversial subject these days, as I remember plain Oxford weave or striped fitted button downs were the order of the day, Ben Sherman, Brutus and Arnold Palmer were the ones to have! A few years later these button downs changed to penny collared or jumbo collared shirts. Jatex and the big bold checks came a lot later in my opinion? Of course Fred Perrys were worn back then too, smart, casual, comfortable and would go with anything! My school uniform at the time was a bit special: White Ben Sherman button down, school tie with a somewhat impossibly large knot, black tank top, Barrathea blazer, black Levi's Sta-Prest and black loafers. Thought I looked a bit 'arry and of course I had the attitude to match!

Like I said I was in the 1st year. The 3rd, 4th and 5th year students looked like men, proper grown ups with facial hair and what seemed like loads of money to spend on all the latest gear, to go to any of the many 'Unisex' hairdressers popping up in Medway rather than just going to the barbers like the rest of us (I'd only just got out of being dragged to the barbers by the Old Man about a year previously, short back and sides with a large dollop of Vitalis to smooth the top in place). The Hygenic in Bachelor Street or Chatham bogs was where I got my barnet cut, seemed ridiculously short at the time but not by today's standards!

All this happened about the same time as I gave up playing football and making Airfix model kits because all of a sudden all I could think of was girls, not just the way they looked but also the way they smelt, everyone and I mean everyone that was anyone, male or female were smothering themselves in Brut 33 and I was no exception. This was before they did the gift packs and the soap on a rope and the deodorant etc etc., all they did were these little bottles of aftershave that didn't seem to last very long for some strange reason? (We were literally bathing in the stuff) (later on Henry Cooper told us to "splash it on all over" not a good idea because before one less than memorable date I splashed it all over and nearly burned my dick off with it!!!).

Couple of things I do remember from back then but I don't know if they were localised or a national things (I've never heard anyone else talking about 'em?). Loafers, you'd go and buy a brand new pair and take them straight down the local snob and have extra leather soles put on with quarter plates front and rear making them very heavy and very noisy especially if you'd gone to town on them and nailed loads of Blakeys in the bottom of them too! And the other thing is about Crombies, girls used to go down to Woolies and buy cutsey patches, butterflies or teddy bears or bunny rabbits and sew them on the breast pocket below the handkerchief and tie stud. Us chaps (remember, this was back in the day before you could buy your favourite football club shirts, you could buy the shirt colour of choice, mine being of the claret and blue variety, but they weren't badged up like they are today), you could buy some football badges (the larger more popular clubs) from certain sports shops, these were embroidered on a piece of white cotton about 5" square, these were sewn (in its entirety) onto the Crombie breast pocket, again below the silk hankie and tie pin.

The girls back then, apart from the tonic skirts and the tights with the patterns down the sides wore pretty much what we wore, but they looked so much better in it than we did. The fitted shirts fitted better, the Sta-Prest seemed to show off their curves a treat too! But it was the hair that did it for me, feathered hair; I don't mean the Chelsea crop of latter years but the proper long feathered hair! It was a much softer, girly look back then, one that I've still got a soft spot for all these years later.

Nigel Harris.

★ ★ ★

Interview with Jonathan Freedman, owner of Brutus

Interviewer: How did you take over the Brutus Trimfit?
Jonathan: I was born into it really. It was always a part of my childhood. At an early age I would go out with my dad (Keith) and buy samples and often during school holidays I would go to the offices and spend time with the designers. I enjoyed it, I saw it as fun. And then about five years ago I started to research the brand. I mean, my dad had kept nothing at all, no shirts, jeans, he didn't have an archive at all. So I made use of the internet and started my research. It was during this exploring that I came across a Brutus Trimfit shirt that I discovered had been mentioned by people and in some books. There was even one in the Museum of London representing an example of an icon of British history. I was fascinated with what I discovered. I mean I was born in 1980 and the Trimfit went back to 1967.

So I found a Trimfit shirt on Ebay and bought it (after a bidding war that eventually set me back over a hundred quid). And then I bought three or four more after that. I would show them to my dad and he would tell me the story behind each piece. There was always a story behind every item, whether it was a shirt or a pair of jeans.

I found that I became more interested and then almost obsessed by it all and found myself trying to hunt down as many pieces of the clothing as I could. It was like I wanted to find out about my heritage that I knew very little about. So I guess that is how the Brutus Trimfit re-launch started.

Very early on Paolo Hewitt came to meet with me and my dad. Paolo did an interview and I remembered that he told me a story of writing an essay about Brutus whilst at school. It all helped and then I set up a Facebook page called Brutus Trimfit and within a couple of weeks there was like a thousand people on there talking about the brand and sending in photographs and the whole thing just kind of snowballed really.

So then I went and had three original Trimfit shirts made. There were based exactly on the shirts that I had bought from off Ebay. That was one of the important things I wanted to keep the shirts exact and original. The purists that love the shirt often say that you can always spot a Brutus by the things like the roll in its collar or by the V in the sleeve and so on, it was never about a label or logo being advertised. And to me this was all important so I decided to keep the new range true to its original design.

That's part of the shirt's charm.
Jonathan: Yes that is part of its charm and it kept the purists on side too which I wanted. I mean there are something like 9000 members on the Facebook site now and as soon as I post some news up so many of them post a reply. They are very pro-active fans and I have really learnt a lot from them.

So then it got more serious. I took over the brand. I mean the ownership was spread across various members of my family so I didn't have to seek out who owned the copyright and so on. Over the years there have been various people who have approached my dad or uncle trying to buy the name, you know, like what happened with Fred Perry and Ben Sherman, but my family never wanted to sell it and I always said 'don't sell it, don't sell it because one day we'll do something with it'.

And so that is what I did. I got a few shirts made up. My dad took me out to the Far East to the original place where the shirts were made. Once I had the samples I took them to shops that I thought were relevant to the brand like Jump the Gun in Brighton and Stuarts in Shepherds Bush. I also went to Oi Poloi in Manchester too to get that mix of outlets that would market the shirts to the purists and also the new people that would know anything about the original Brutus.

There was some feedback where people were saying things like, 'Look, we're all a bit bigger now, so why don't you make the shirts a big looser?' but my response was always along the lines of 'Why should we change anything about the shirt. The Trimfit was designed for 15 and 16 year old kids and that's what we want to do again.' And my attitude on this hasn't changed since day one. But we have found a way to hit both markets.

There was times at the start where I would be phoning people up and saying that I was re-launching Brutus and often the response would be, 'Eh, what is Brutus?' but then there was others that identified with it straight away.

So I managed to get the first three shirts out which were the black and white check, the red and white check and the blue and white check. These three shirts ran for about twelve months before we introduced additional ranges. I was still buying shirts from Ebay and as soon as I got them I was having them made. There was a point where I was launching a new shirt via Facebook every other month and they were selling out in like 24 hours.

I also found I was getting busier with the Facebook page to and so then set up an online store. The Trimfits were also selling well in Germany. They have a massive scene out there for our style of shirts. And then sales were coming from Japan, Australia and Russia. It's amazing that in this day you can kind of launch a brand by yourself using mostly the internet.

How many do you have in your team?
Jonathan: Me. I mean, I do use a PR company and the warehousing is out-sourced. I will take on an assistant at some point though.

I do have my dad and family behind me. My dad is very helpful. He is glad that I have done it. He understands that the marketing side of the business is different now. I mean now we don't have to do television or cinema ads. But essentially the business side is the same and I love it. It started out as a kind of a hobby for me and now I just love it.

At the start of 2012 we collaborated with Doc Martens. We designed a shirt including a colour based on the Oxblood boot and the yellow of their stitching and added a bespoke label Brutus for Doc Martens. The shirt was sold through 26 of Doc Martens' flagship stores across the world. Again, the shirts sold out within 24 hours across the world. In fact Doc Martens told me that it was the first time in Doc Martens history that people were walking into the stores asking for a shirt and not a boot.

There is also the new Brutus jean range launched in 2013. We are using a Japanese denim. The cut is very clean and we using elements of the original Brutus Gold range. So the Gold bar will be included, the buttons and rivets too. I actually like the idea of retailing them at sixty six pounds because that was the year when Brutus was founded. I also want to keep the cost low so that we don't lose our current Brutus customers. I really don't want to start including pieces that retail for like two hundred and fifty quid like so many other makes of jeans. I never feel the need to want to rip anybody off.

We also have a range of '70s style shirts that we are working on. The only difference is that we will manufacture the 70's shirts in a Trimfit style and exclude the massive pointy collars. These shirts may become popular with the Northern Soul scene.

So a bit of Brutus history. Where was the original office?
Jonathan: The first offices were located on the Commercial Road down in the East End. Following this there were offices and warehouses that followed in Haringey and then onto Wigmore Street. My dad and his brother were from the East End area.

My grandfather (Harry Freedman) was a general wholesaler in the East End, so he basically sold anything and everything. At some point he sold workman's polo necks that only came in the colours black and brown. My dad asked his dad if he could get them made in white. My dad had the notion that he could sell the white polos to a few fashion stores in places like Carnaby Street. So some white versions were made and my dad managed to sell them in these fashion stores. They became very much a fashion item amongst the young people of the time.

So then my dad decided to start to get some of the garments made up himself and found some firm in Hong Kong who began to make them. This was in 1965. My dad was seventeen.

Then Brutus as a brand came around in 1966. And it's true that the name derived from the aftershave Brut because that was the aftershave that my dad used. Although, I will add that I have never got a 100% story about it out of my dad.

So my dad and his brother would go to Hong Kong a few times a year and return with these knitwear items. It was very hot in Hong Kong and it was also the same time as the Vietnam war. The American soldiers who were on R&R would be down Nathan Road wearing these short sleeve Brooks Brothers button down style shirts. My dad noticed them and even bought some himself. But he found that they were boxy and big and typical American-style shirts and when he returned to the UK and tried to sell them to retailers they commented on the shape and size and said they wouldn't sell to British Kids. This was a time when the Mods were on the hunt for good clothes. But they were sixteen year old kids who wanted their shirts tight and fitted.

In response, my dad had some shirts made with the required adjustments, the darts and pleats and the two button feature on the V on the sleeve. And the Brutus Trimfit shirt was born. The jeans didn't start being made until the early '70s. My dad and his brother found a factory that could wash jeans, which at the time was kind of unheard of. The first batch of washed denim jeans arrived and the story goes was that they were all mouldy due to having not been dried properly. It was early days and people just didn't know enough. Brutus kind of developed the idea of washed jeans. Then came the flares that got bigger and bigger and then came the patches, the embroidery and so on. The biggest selling range during the late '70s was the Brutus Gold. Millions of Golds were sold.

The '70s was also a time where the shirts changed. Brutus stopped doing the checks and started introducing shirts with prints on them, big collars. The '70s wanted things 'loud'. I have heard that on the Northern Soul scene the Casino etc that the preferred choice was a '60s Brutus shirt and this was mixed with Brutus (or another brand's) flared jeans for example.

The '80s was a time of change. Many retailers were going bust and Brutus had to respond to this change in business. By the time the early '90s arrived my dad started to get into the property business and also my grandfather died. My grandfather had always been very involved in the development of the company and much of Brutus was associated with him. It was the combination of these factors really brought the Brutus brand to a close and that's how it stayed until I picked it up again in 2007.

Jonathan Freedman.

★ ★ ★

Nicky Porter, Skinhead girl.

It all began in a leafy outer suburb of London. The year was 1977. I remember the day like it was yesterday. I had taken the bus to a salon in Hounslow as my usual hairdresser had refused to cut my long auburn hair off! I had asked for a boyish cut, the stylist called it the 'Elfin' look, and basically it was a crop. My parents returned from their holiday in France. The reaction was not good. I can't remember how many weeks it took my dad to look at me. My mother, to this day, blames Johnny Rotten. Punk had arrived.

We became creative, painting shirts with "God Save the Queen" and hunting Oxfam shops for granny style clothing to go with our old school blazers. We altered our jeans so they became drain-pipes and teamed them with plastic sandals or winkle pickers. I started listening to live music following friend's bands The Dials and The Wardens.

Around this time we all went to the Winning Post in Whitton. It was 8th June, 1977. Three sharply dressed young punks came on stage. Awkwardly, the lead singer introduced the band, "Good evening, we are The Jam" followed by "1, 2, 3!" and the most exciting raw sound I had ever heard. We followed them to several gigs after that, The Nashville Rooms, Hammersmith Odeon and Bracknell Sports Centre to name a few. Little did I realise then that, nearly 35 years later, I would still be listening to Weller's music and loving it. Punk and New Wave had hit the streets. Weekends were spent on buses and the tube searching obscure bands in London pubs, 999, The Rezillos, Milk, Buzzcocks, Penetration, Generation X, The Clash and X Ray Spex to name a few. I was lucky to be at the *Top of the Pops* studio when X Ray Spex performed and I saw myself on the tele when it was screened on the 18th May, 1978.

On Friday 5th May we attended the Coronation Hall in Kingston upon Thames to see Sham 69 play. It was to be a memorable night. A small group of trouble makers spilled into the streets after a tense gig. Pleas from Jimmy to calm down had fallen on deaf ears. That night the route from the hall to the train station was a dangerous one to be on. The small disruptive group became more aggressive and destructive as they ran through the streets, kicking out at vehicles and anything or anyone that got in their way. In the pouring rain the sound of crashing glass and sirens echoed out. Dozens of pairs of jeans were being looted, single shoes lay in the puddles in the road promptly driven over by the buses and police vans. My favourite jeans store had been emptied.

Elmbridge Council barred the band from performing at its halls. It didn't stop them playing many more times, even America, with the final gig (1979) ending in the usual violence at Middlesex Poly. It was about this time that Two-Tone had taken off. The Nashville Rooms on the corner of the Cromwell Road at West Kensington was a popular place. I think the first time I saw The Specials was here in June 79. It cost £1 to get in! It was a great venue, a large room adjacent to the pub and it was here that I saw Madness. 1979 was the year of change for me. My parents and sister, who shared my love of music, left for America for a year and I became an art student in Epsom.

The music movements were developing. Where once you found mods, punks and skin bands on the same line-up, now they were diverging. I was listening to more reggae and ska and original sounds from around the late '60s. I began to collect rare vinyl imports from Jamaica guided by the old hippy on his stall in Kingston market, Trojan, Pama and Treasure Isle were some favourite labels.

My obsession with charity shops and flea markets became a refined search for original Sta-Prest, Ben Shermans and Brutus. I found my Crombie in an Oxfam in Epsom High Street. It was a deep dark navy almost black and a perfect fit. Kingston station had a 'gentlemen's outfitters that sold red tab Levi's. The original shrink to fit. I remember sitting in the bath until my legs had gone blue, from the dye not the cold! We altered the length of our jeans with a minimal turn-up, ¼ inch, displaying the pale inner denim and the red and white edge. The shop was popular with the teddy boys and rockabillies and had many coloured drape-coats on the rails. Alongside the suede creepers they stocked Frank Wright shoes, loafers, brogues and smooths. I had a pair of these loafers in black with tassles. I wore oxblood monkey boots in the day at college. When we got dressed up for a night out I preferred my highly polished penny loafers, also oxblood red. I always bought the same make. They were expensive but worth it from The Natural Shoe Store on the Kings Road. They were an American make, Bass, with a stitched leather sole. They were a more feminine loafer and perfect with a tonic jacket and skirt. We'd always add metal blakeys to the heel. I also continued to search Kensington Market. In the punk days when we were looking for something a bit different we came here. I became the proud owner of many checked shirts, all original Ben Shermans, some Brutus. A good friend, Belinda, later sourced, I think from one of the vintage markets, white ribbed tights with a keyhole detail down the outside of the leg. I think we were the only ones to wear them on the scene.

It was when I went to Art School that I made some new friends that shared my passion for clothes and music of this style, one of whose sister had been an original skinhead in 69. She kindly gave me her original petrol blue and gold tonic jacket, it had been hand-made for her. This fed my obsession and soon I owned 4 or 5 tonic jackets and coats, all slightly different but with the all important detailing of the fabric covered tiny buttons. I inherited tie and hat pins from my grandma, my favourite was a butterfly which was a popular theme in the late '60s early '70s. I also had a good selection of silk hankies for the top pocket, perfectly folded to 3 points and occasionally a paisley scarf to finish off the look.

I moved in to a flat with Sharon, a fellow art student. She shared my love of this era and of Northern Soul. Together we had an amazing record collection. I continued to see my old mates and at weekends we met at Feltham Football Club. Skins and punks mixed well here and often a live band played. If not, local boy Tony Curtis would DJ playing a great mix of ska, reggae and punk. Other times we would take the train to Clapham Junction walking through a dodgy estate to The York Tavern. Skinheads from all over London and further would meet here. It was one of the few pubs where we could all meet up and were accepted, enjoying a drink and listening to our music. It was a popular place, quickly filling up and spilling onto the streets.

We continued to shop at the second-hand markets. There were quite a few in the Kings Road, Chelsea, and it had always been a good place to meet new faces. Bank Holidays were spent on long train journeys to various seaside destinations. Often on arrival, because of our 'look', we would be put straight back on a train for London by the police. The Skinhead revival sadly was getting a bad reputation.

My four years at Art School had come to an end. I moved back to my parents' home in Sunbury and got a job at Normansfield Hospital, the start of a career, I hoped, in art therapy. Around this time my sister had a new boyfriend with a Lambretta. Not long after we joined him on 2 wheels. Our newly acquired Vespas took us to fresh venues and we began to enjoy a scene free from the racism and violence that was growing in other areas.

On a Wednesday I would occasionally go to a club in Kingston, at the back of the old Bentalls store, for a night of soul and ska. The Shepherd's Bush Hotel was popular on a Sunday night at Sneakers, the club run by Paul Hallam, a local boy from our home town of Sunbury. It was here that I met Mr Extraordinary Sensations and was promptly nicknamed 'Suedehead'! My barber in Epsom had always given me a scissor cut, probably the equivalent of a No.4 with a carefully layered longer fringe and neck. Now it had grown into an authentic feather cut brushed off the forehead to one side. I dressed accordingly adding a paisley Ben Sherman, tank tops and a Fair Isle yolk neck jumper to my wardrobe, always worn with one of my tonic jackets.

Sneakers and The Phoenix became regular fixtures. The mod scene was full on, always somewhere to go with new clubs popping up all over and bands to like, Makin Time and The Untouchables to go and see. Scooter rallies took us to the coast and the Isle of Wight for long weekends away. Back in London we would meet for cappuccinos in Carnaby Street by day before deciding which club to go to that evening. Sometimes we would travel to north London to meet up with the Camden Stylists. They too shared my obsession with authenticity and tonic and a love of ska. It was here in Camden at Dingwalls that we danced the night away to Desmond Dekker. That was around 84/85.

Now all these years later I still have my prized record collection and listening to the old sounds still makes me smile. I sold my wardrobe, in a weak moment to my old friend Belinda, keeping my favourite green and gold tonic coat. I still wear Levi's. I have a better scooter now, thanks to my husband, a fully restored Lambretta LI 150 Silver Special. I live a quieter life and on a sunny day can be seen out riding in New Zealand, remembering the good old days.

Nicky Porter (formerly Locking).

★ ★ ★

Gavin Watson: 'An Explanation' – Extracted from his classic photography book, Skins.

I am the dreaded middle child, the place in the family that seems to breed the black sheep.

I was 13 when I bought my very first camera. I got it from Woolworths and it was called a Hanimex. I'd got some Christmas money and had decided I wanted to buy either a camera or a pair of binoculars. I'd decided on the binoculars – I can't remember why – but when I got to Woolworths, there was a sale on and the camera was cheaper, so I got that. By chance, this little camera had a glass lens, so the first photographs I got back were crystal clear and sharp and when I saw them something happened inside of me and I just thought, *I want this, I want to take pictures.* It was a very powerful moment.

There were no professional photographers in my family; my brother Mark took lots of pictures and my dad was a frustrated artist and musician who was working very hard as an engineer in the middle of nowhere. I was an introverted kid who'd been diagnosed with severe dyslexia at the age of eight and had suspected borderline Asperger's syndrome. I was a shy child, living in my own virile fantasy world. That was a lot more exciting and in a way more real than my reality, which wasn't much cop. Dyslexic, painfully shy, trouble at home. Unhappy parents. When I talk about my childhood to some of my mates, their instant reaction is, it can't have been that bad.

Suddenly, all I wanted to do was take pictures.

My nature is obsessive, meticulous, so I voraciously began to consume everything and anything about photography. My dad saw the pictures I was taking and took a great interest in that and in me. He bought me this Zenit TTL which was this cheap single lens reflex camera that you could change the lenses on. So I used that for a little while, then the skinhead thing came in and my dad bought me an Olympus OM1, which caused quite a lot of contention in the family because there were three kids to feed, clothe and get to school and that was a very expensive camera. At the time, it was very uncomfortable for me – I remember opening the box in the kitchen and the shock on the faces of my brothers and mom contrasted so much with the pride of my dad, and me … I wasn't used to getting any attention, I was used to spending all the time on my own.

The year before I even became a skinhead, I had long hair, I was into cheesy disco and Gary Numan, I was a total div when I got those first cameras. I wasn't hanging out with the skinhead friends you see in my book yet. I was always very artistic and loved to draw and paint so I always loved art at school. I believe that the rudiments I learnt in art class – especially the lessons about perspective – have been cornerstones behind my photography. The more I look at my early work, the more I believe that I must have had some subconscious form of artistic influence from the art class even though it must have been very covert at the time. Even though I dreamt of my pictures being in *National Geographic*, I had no photographic heroes. What I learnt as a photographer is what I taught myself.

I became a skinhead because of the music and the attention I received, especially from girls. I loved dancing, music and girls, and the Two Tone scene seemed to have it all. It totally spoke to me about my environment which was the new generation of the multi-cultural kids that were coming of age, Jamaicans, Irish, etc.

Wycombe Skins.

There were about twenty of us, all mongrel dogs from a pretty grim estate called Micklefield in a town called High Wycombe that's in Buckinghamshire, causing mischief and mayhem round town. Yet somehow, even though I was in this amazing, unique gang, I always felt like a misfit, even as a skinhead there was a nagging feeling that I did not fit in. That's what this whole thing is about, not fitting in to others' expectations.

I carried my camera with me everywhere. People mostly don't have an understanding of the nature of my archive. There are thousands of images, potent, you can trawl through them for days. But at the time, there was a very real financial limitation. I'd joined a little camera club this bloke ran in the evenings and he taught me and my friend Simon how to process films, that's where the black and white stuff started coming in. As an engineer, my dad took a great interest in that aspect of it, so he got the proper equipment to process my negs and he'd do so as an engineer. So I'd go out and take these pictures and he would process them perfectly in the house. That would never have happened without him.

We couldn't really do too much printing, it was too expensive, but my dad was always processing these negatives for me. This went on for about a year, processing the negs, and I would try and get the odd print done here and there, maybe at school or through a make-shift dark room that we cobbled together in the bathroom.

When it came down to film, I obviously couldn't afford much. I have never been very good with money, it's always been an issue. So I would go into Boots and get a film and sometimes that would have to last me a month. It had to last, so my pictures had to count. That said, I sometimes used to get a mate to go and steal films from the front of the shop. But essentially, I had to really think about every picture I took.

Locally, I became known for carrying my camera but somehow it didn't seem to bother anybody. I was so insular in my head, so innocent, I seemed to be able to wander into a gang of dangerous, 18-year-old skinheads and take these pictures. I just had that way about me, that's what I seemed to do.

Before I knew it, I found myself with 3,000-plus images from that specific period and have a further 10,000 on my life growing up as a skinhead in England in the '80s, plus the work I have done in the music industry, the rave scene and the thousands I have taken in the course of my general life.

The stories are the most important thing. The stories, the myths, the memories, that's what all this is really about, memories of the time when you were young and didn't give a fuck... or a least pretended you didn't.

The boy on the front cover of *Skins* giving the two fingers is my younger brother Neville. My father once opened the door to a gang of skins in their twenties, asking if Neville – who was still in primary school – was coming to hang out? What effect this had on a ten-year-old boy – not to mention the effect it must have had on Dad – I sometimes wonder. Neville was the perfect height for all those lovely girls who thought he was the sweetest thing they'd ever seen and had to give him a big hug to prove it.

He must have had more breasts shoved into his face than any of us hormone raging teenagers could have hoped for. Neville became a mascot.

Neville, I must confess, was used by us as we cruised round town looking for members of the opposite sex. He always received such a lot of attention from girls that we hoped some of that glory would reflect onto us. I don't think it ever really worked, but we made a lot of friends.

The famous cover shot of Neville sticking up his two fingers was taken in the autumn. I think I had just got the Olympus. It was after school and I knew Nev was hanging out up at the playground in the Micklefield estate. I went up there to test the camera out with my brother and his little mate for a couple of hours, it was no special occasion, that was just the key shot of that afternoon. The neg sheet from that day provided me with a few photos, indeed many of my afternoons spent taking photographs produced several pictures in this book on the same contact sheet. I had to be very careful.

People have often commented that my mates in the pictures seem very relaxed, they are not self-conscious and how did I get that? I just hung out with my camera and I'd see a picture and I'd take it. They were my mates. They were skins and into fashion so they were poseurs but it is a difficult question to answer, no one ever questioned that I had the camera. I would make up a print in the bathroom, a nice black and white picture and give it to somebody, hand it to the person in the picture and they were not used to it, they loved it.

These photographs were taken at a time in the late '70s when a lot of confusion was being expressed by the youth as Mods, skinheads, rastas, rudeboys, rockers, punks, Nazis, anti-Nazis etc, all made their statements. Over the years, I have been asked too many times about the right-wing aspects of skinhead culture but [that] book is not about that, it is a book of photographs. What I will say is that when I was in the middle of doing interviews about the first edition, I was always asked about racism – even though my pictures and life show a divergent and definite cultural mix. Yet it always seemed to be a middle class ex-college student with luke-warm Marxist ideals; never was I asked about racism by a black or Asian writer.

It makes perfect sense to me why the kids in these pictures – and in Britain at that time – went around and did the things that so confused the older generation: they were just trying to deal with massive shifts in society. The promise of a rich and glamorous, as-seen-on-TV life was everywhere, the new opium, as against a harsher reality and bleak future that looked incredibly dull compared to what these other people had, you know, those 'perfect people' on the box. The perfect family ideal of a little house on the prairie or the rich sophistication of *Dallas*. I don't think people realise the power of these images or how many people are still carrying inside them the dream that one day they will be living the high life of JR Ewing. The more grim the surroundings, the more these dreams and glamorous images become the only hope of young people living in depressed circumstances. The problem was that it quickly became apparent there weren't many opportunities to climb out of poverty.

Before that time, I discovered that it was my cat and fossil-hunting that kept me sane... those two things and photography.

The god of photography was obviously on my side because just before I was sixteen I looked in the back of *Amateur Photographer* and there was this tiny little advert for a dark room assistant at Camera Press in London, one of the biggest and most famous agencies in the world. It was six months before I had to leave school but I just phoned 'em up, went for the interview and got the job. I went to school and said, 'Look, I've got this job!' and they said, 'Well, you ain't doing any good here, mate, you might as well take it.' Suddenly I was in this dark room surrounded by photographs by Karsh, Lichfield and Snowdon, all the great names. And, of course, now I could process my own film myself.

Tom Blau ran the place from a flat above this old building where the basement had the dark room. I was sixteen. Kids were thinking about getting a job at the post office or in a factory or something and there was me taking these pictures.

What made me take all these pictures in the first place was a personal compulsion. I did have a strong sense of time and destiny. As a kid of 14, I clearly thought, I have got to record this. I felt that very, very strongly, that there was something really special about this and obviously there was. Not in that youthful way that lots of 14-year-old kids think their gang is great, there was something important about this gang, there was a special moment going on, something working through me to take those pictures.

It's hard to explain, but that's how I felt.

People often ask me why these pictures taken by a child have such lasting resonance all these years later. For me, it is because they are so potent. That's the only word that springs to mind: potent. But if I am totally honest, it is difficult when you are the creator of something like this to judge it and comment on it, especially when you were only a child when you created it. Some of my shots are now considered iconic classics and that removes my personality from it anyway, because they will still be there when I am dead and gone.

The reason for [this Introduction to my book] is that I felt I had an obligation to explain a bit about the story behind *Skins*. The lack of explanation was deliberate in the first edition of the book. I wanted the photography to speak for itself, which I feel worked, to some extent. I hope these words go some way to explaining a little bit more detail about events in my life that led to the book. However, the book remains, first and foremost, a photographic record.

My name is Gavin Watson.

I was born in Kingsbury, London on September 7, 1965.

My mother was from Ireland, my dad came from Palmers Green in north London.

The family moved from London to Aylesbury, Buckingham-shire, when I was about three and then onto High Wycombe, Bucks, when I was six.

I have two brothers, Mark who is three-and-a-half years my senior, and Neville, who is three-and-a-half years my junior ... me being the dreaded middle child, the place in the family that seems to breed the black sheep.

Gavin Watson.

★ ★ ★

The thoughts of an original 1969 skinhead, Chris Weeks.

I was born in Plumbstead and then brought up in Eltham in a house with several other family members including an uncle who use to live under the stairs. In the '50s, a few years after the war everything was still pretty much the same, we wore socks up to the knees with the blue tabs and then in the '60s we got a bit more fashionable and I got my first Brogues. My parents' marriage went pear-shaped and my mum moved to Charlton in a house near the ground. My granddad took me to my first Charlton game when I was 5 years old.

I became a Skinhead in 1969 after I had seen my first Skinhead when I was 14 years old. I remember this fella in Sta-Prest and holding two Ben Sherman shirts and I was in awe and told myself that is what I wanted to be. I left school when I was 14 and went to work at Burtons in Bexley Heath as a junior tailor. That was when I got my first Crombie. That Crombie went with me everywhere, to all the home and away games via Lewis' coaches. It cost me £120 and that was even with the staff discount.

Around the age of 15 I was wearing brown Dr. Martens boots

and we used to use polish to cover up the yellow stitching. I was wearing Ben Shermans, the original shirts only had 2 holes on the buttons. The 4 holes only came later along with the tab on the pocket. We had Brutus shirts which were for the poor man's skinhead, like I was at first. I had a pale blue Ben Sherman, with the dart at the back and the hook. At the time Ben Sherman's were the top shirt, they cost about 19 shillings. Brutus were half the price. We use to get our Brutus from Millett's up in Eltham. We use to go to Petticoat Lane to get the Ben Shermans. The Levi's we had were much better material. My first pair of Levi's cost me 59 shillings. They were not 501s back then, they were just Levi's Sta-Prest. Levi's also had to have a half inch turn up, if you didn't you just wasn't one of the boy's. I remember I was at an away game once and after having a bit of a ruck I got a tear in the knee so I had to take a bit off the bottom and stitch it in the hole. Then we had half inch braces, never an inch. I also had Royals Brogues which you had to wear with white socks which we called Squires. I also had some shoes called Gibson's which were a square toe shoe. They were called Smooths.

At first we use to wear these green Vietnam combat jackets and then they bought out Monkey Jackets. I had a dark blue one with a red, white and blue collar. And then the Harrington's came in but we called them Squires jackets. The original Squires jackets had the tartan lining but they didn't have an inside pocket. The leader of the crew would wear a light colour one because he was like the top boy and the rest of us would wear the black or dark red ones. Our hair was cropped to about a number 2 or 3 and had a small razor cut parting.

Chris Weeks.

TWO TONE

A Rude Boy account from the late '70s by Lee Barden.

Rude boy tales. The summer of 1979 and the newly formed 2 Tone Records released 'Gangsters' by The Specials. Madness appeared on the scene with 'The Prince', this heralded my obsession with Two Tone and Ska music. The music was based on the '60s Jamaican Ska which in England had a big skinhead following. My uncle Herbie was into Ska in the '60s and gave me a bit of a history lesson, so armed with a few facts I set about finding some original recordings. My uncle's mate Kevin Russell had still kept all his old Ska records which were kept in a big old suitcase, there must have been about 300 records. As I started listening to them, the original Ska bug set in. As Two Tone took off, more re-releases come out, *Club Ska 67*, Prince Buster's *Greatest Hits*, *Intensified! Volumes 1 and 2*, *Tighten Up!*, *Catch This Beat*, *The Trojan Story*, all joined my collection. To start with I classed myself as a skinhead, wearing Doc Martens boots, braces, Ben Sherman and Fred Perry shirts, tonic trousers and the Harrington jacket, my uncle give me his Crombie from the '60s and I remember having a silvery grey tonic suit.

Around 1980 I went and saw The Selecter at the Hammersmith Palais, there was about 50 skinheads standing in a big group Sieg Heiling the whole gig and fighting anyone who challenged them. The skinhead movement had always had an element of racism and after I witnessed it I wanted to get well away from it so the move to the Rude Boy culture seemed the best thing to do. The word rude boy originated from Jamaica and meant juvenile delinquent, in this country it was adopted by Two Tone as a name for the followers. At the time in Maidstone most skinheads come from the Shepway estate and trouble always seemed to follow them, I remember going to a party, me, Paul, Leroy, Mark, Cheryl and a few people from Shepway, we all got the bus and was going up the Loose Road when the inspector got on and asked for our tickets. Leroy, a punk from Bearsted, had been chewing his and took it out of his mouth and give it to the inspector who promptly chucked him off the bus. We all followed him, got off the bus then there was an almighty smash, one of the Shepway skins had picked up a rock and threw it through the bus window. We all ran off but didn't get far before a couple of cop cars pulled up and out jumped the coppers and arrested us all, after a few hours in the cells we was charged and let out although most of us had done nothing we still had to go to court, we all got not guilty because when the inspector got asked to point out who threw the rock he more or less said they all looked the same to me, the judge had no evidence and couldn't proceed any further. The first and last time I got in trouble with the police.

The Vinter's girls school disco was the highlight of the month and was full of different fashion groups, you had skinheads, mods, heavies, hippies, punks and rude boys, and a couple of Adam Ant impersonators. Friday night would consist of going to the 'offy', usually opposite Maidstone prison, to buy some cheap cider, get hammered, go to a disco and loon around. On one occasion me and a mate was dancing to 'Concrete Jungle' by The Specials when I saw one of our other mates come in, or so I thought, we both jumped on him and threw him about a bit, when the record finished we realised to our horror it weren't our mate but the local lunatic, thankfully one of our mates knew him and saved us from a beating. [At one disco] I used to take in some original ska tunes and they would play them. I asked them to play 'Madness' by Prince Buster, they said something about you and your mates smashed some of the lights while dancing, the next thing I knew they both started punching me and my mate Paul about the head, with this other people bundled in and chaos ensued. The headmistress stopped the discos, so me and few others got the blame. Discos at other places like the youth club were good but trouble always seemed to be not far around the corner and in the end most of these discos faded out.

The Specials and Madness were having quite a bit of success in the charts, new groups were appearing like The Beat, the Body Snatchers, Bad Manners, reggae sounding, UB40, Dexy's Midnight Runners, but as all good things it had to come to an end. Jerry Dammers steered well clear of the ska influence for the Specials' 2nd album, although a good LP, the raw sound of The Specials LP had gone. Madness had gone for a more poppy sound, The Selecter steered away from Ska and before you knew it everything seemed different. The Specials hit No. 1 with 'Ghost Town' and split not long after; Jerry Dammers carried on for one more album with a new singer but it was never the same and before you knew it the whole thing was finished. Thirty years down the line The Specials reformed without Jerry Dammers and went on a sold-out tour. Madness split and reformed for Madstock and still sound as good today as ever. Looking back I'm glad I was around to witness the rebirth of Ska and meet people I wouldn't have otherwise, good times.

Lee Barden.

★ ★ ★

Jonathan Young: 2 Tone & musical tribes, from then to now.

In 1979 Punk was dead and the nation was craving another musical direction. It came for me in the form of 2 Tone music: the dawning of a new era in the UK's musical and cultural heritage. One of those 'once in a lifetime' things I find hard to explain, sitting bored ignoring the TV and then I heard 'Gangsters' come on. The combination of style, music and politics packaged by 2 Tone became a driving force in my life, and seeing The Specials live was like an explosion 3 inches in front of my face, for their energy. Great reviews brought in crowds and created the scene so quickly.

2 Tone Records was founded by Jerry Dammers. His aim was to create a British record label equivalent to Motown. Based in Coventry, 2 Tone released ska and reggae-influenced music with punk rock and pop music overtones. It changed the face of British music. The artwork that was to make 2 Tone Records immediately identifiable was the famed black and white check and the 'Walt Jabsco' logo, which became iconic. The logo portrayed a man in a black suit, white shirt, black tie, pork pie hat, white socks and black loafer shoes. It was based on a photograph of Peter Tosh, a former member of reggae legend Bob Marley's band The Wailers. The logo was named Walt Jabsco after the name on a bowling shirt owned by Jerry Dammers at the time. The images became as famous as the bands and their music.

2 Tone swept the UK with an unprecedented fervour, they also signed other like-minded bands: The Selecter, Madness, The Beat, The Bodysnatchers and The Swinging Cats. Other Midlands artists such as Dexys Midnight Runners, UB40 & Bad Manners flirted with joining the 2 Tone label.

For 3 years, when I was a teenager, the nation danced under the chequered flag and enjoyed many 2Tone hits. The label also had a serious message, adopted by all of us who followed the music, the whole black and white theme, with its anti-racist ideology, gave the youth a voice to listen to. The country was awash with kids all in one big family. Songs included tales of tolerance and harmony and at a time when the UK's political arena had seen the rise of the far right groups on a national scale. The label would influence a new generation of artists to form their own bands and continue to spread the racial harmony message of 2Tone long after the original bands departed in new directions. Not before 'Ghost Town' reached number one and perfectly captured the times as a snapshot of race riots, unemployment, dwindling town centre recession and disenfranchised youth.

It was gutting when the split came, it felt like having your voice taken away at the time. Then in the press 2Tone faded, I started Ska nights that became more and more popular, and my fanzine on 2Tone showed there was interest still out there and international interest too in the label. Later ST publishing was instrumental in circulating books about these bands, and reprinting old Richard Allen skinhead novels, which kept the interest going into the '90s.

2Tone was a starting out point for Madness, who quickly developed their own career One Step Beyond it. The 2Tone bands all separated quite early on and continued to then have hits or off-shoots, but via discographies fans continue to find their way back to the beginning of these band's stories. The seminal LP was *Dance Craze*, it told you with its tracklisting and with the simple fact that every band on the black and white cover had a kind of badge symbol, that these acts were linked and this was a style movement.

Those a few years too young to be around 2Tone as a teenager, like I was, tended to then look up to siblings or people older in school who were talking about such topics glamourously.

My sister was old enough to experience The Specials & Madness as they first arrived, through her *Top of the Pops* devotion and tape recorder to TV speaker bootlegging of tracks, (with occasional audio interruptions from her bratty little brother coughing). I got the bug second-hand through our first home video recorder (Betamax) introducing me to Madness via the revolutionary sitcom *The Young Ones* taped by my dad. Then we scoured record fairs together. The lack of further information around in the late '80s early '90s led me into fanzine culture, which is where I first found a music scene becoming a social way of mixing with all sorts of people and forming friendships, all around the time of The Madstock Madness comeback gigs which were a spine-tingling celebration of the return of the Magnificent Seven. They stood on stage as seven, arms raised at the start of those concerts and were adored by a wave of affection palpable from the crowd. These fans were now people I was sharing seminal moments with and that's what links any group of people together.

There's always been a mix of Skinhead, Suedehead, ska fans, Fred Perry, Mod, and more general music fans that follow this band, those gigs in the '90s were very much a sub-culture soup! Weirdly it included Ravers with Flowered Up appearing at the first Madstock and Suggs having one toe in the Hacienda scene through his work with The Farm. Fez's or Swag (a mix of demob suits and Americana and shades) or nutty dressing though are just as likely from a Tommy Cooper to Pythonesque British sense of humour, as anything that is linked to a love of Jamaican tunes past was.

The internet changed everything for subcultures and music fans in the late '90s. Fanzine runners like Paul or contributors like myself now had speedy electronic ways to share their stories and band information, from mailing lists, through forums and myriad tribute websites that would spring up. Specials2 and Madness Information Service Online were born from these times. Band appreciation and meeting fellow fans surged massively and with full on enthusiasm, it was a starved underground interest resurging and a second generation joining in. This lead to gatherings and weekenders. The term Mad–Meet coined for pilgramages to Camden Town and The Dublin Castle, and Blackpool through to Minehead was taken over for fancy dressed lunacy and celebration, apeing the videos of Madness at weekenders, very much a jolly nutty boys outing. Cross over interest in The Specials from some more active Madness fans came much later in 2009 when that band's line-up also reformed to great reactions.

The sense of community that Jerry Dammers once instilled in 1979 can still unite fans now in unique ways. Both Madness and The Specials supported Teenage Cancer as a charity of choice through Roger Daltrey's music projects at the Albert Hall in the last decade. This led to fans' communities focussing on Specialized, as one example.

As the admin of the Specials online fan club, I needed to think of a way of keeping the band's profile on the high whilst they were preparing to take time off from touring. I hit on the idea of using the Specials name incorporated with a project I decided to call Specialized (the Z being for effect, not USA spelling!). A fundraising project with modern acts covering Specials songs (subsequently leading to 2 other albums of covering songs by The Beat & Madness), it was to be self-funded by likeminded individuals to press physical albums. I intended to run it in the ethos and spirit of 2Tone and I think I do that to good effect. It's a community matter and concern. We were told, through song lyrics and interviews by the 2Tone bands back in the heyday ,that we could do anything if we wanted to put our minds to it and I think Specialized encompasses that. And, as did 2Tone, it has captured hearts and minds across the ska community and beyond. Now widened to include a project on The Clash after already raising over £75,000 with the first three covers albums and many other projects in the name of these inspirational bands."

Now more than 35 years on, fandom of 2Tone music is still

strong, at a time when we find ourselves linked to everyone & their aunt's dog through social media so easily, the tribal headings are much less the focus, fandoms have shifted and 2Tone exists more as a topic, linking people in discussion, on top of old networks that continue to grow, while the avatar experience is now a more immediate show-and-tell element, getting ever more personal around it all. A tweet, a vid or a selfie with a band member or an autograph, is all nuttyness in a nutshell now. But projects like Specialized show how deep and wide music topics can be shared so quickly, for important reasons still, with involvement and new spin-offs happening in what seems a smaller more immediate world.

www.specializedproject.co.uk
Paul Williams – www.thespecials2.com
Jonathan Young – www.madness-mis.com

★ ★ ★

Rude Boy Richard Lambert.

I was a rude boy between 1981 and 1982, I was 11 years old. I loved Madness and The Beat (as well as Dexy's Midnight Runners and The Jam). I had a pair of Frank Wright loafer's, which I wore with white towelling socks. I was also a member of the Madness 'nutty boys' fan club.

Being a Rude Boy at 11 years of age meant there was a uniform and a look that could be easily copied. I wanted to copy the older boys at school. The 'cool' older kids were all Rude Boys or Mods, the ones that I used to look up to. There wasn't any Rude Boys in the small Kentish village where I grew up and I think this was part of the appeal. My older sister used to take me to a local church youth club. It was called the Monday Nighters and the 't' in the Nighters on the club sweatshirts was the symbol of the cross. Most of the young people who went to the club listened to Queen or Peter Gabriel. 'Bohemian Rapsody' would often be sung on the minibus to club outings or activities.

School was the place to be a Rude Boy. I had a friend in my class, Ian, who was a mod and we would constantly talk about the clothes and the music. He knew a lot of the older boys at school because he had an older sister. My friendship with Ian meant that I was acknowledged or tolerated by the older mods and Rude Boys. I remember being tested by an older kid one lunchtime about my Rude Boy credentials, I was asked about my knowledge of the music, I was able to talk about ska, two tone and blue beat. I seemed to pass the test and I didn't get the piss taken out of me.

I wore my Frank Wright loafers to School and had a metal quarter tip put into the heel and the thin part of the tie on show, the fat part tucked into my shirt. I didn't have my head shaved but had short hair and a centre parting. I don't think my parents would have allowed me to have a skinhead or Suedehead. I remember my dad taking me to Huckel's Men's clothes shop in Maidstone to buy my School trousers. I wanted a pair of Sta-Prest but my dad bought me some grey woolen flairs. I was devastated, I knew I couldn't go to school wearing a pair of 'Lionels' and was so upset when I got home that my mum sent my dad back out to exchange them and get the ones I wanted. The Sta-Prest sold in Huckle's were made by Ziggy's and had an orange 'z' label above the front right trouser pocket.

Huckle's stocked all the gear, Sta-Prest, Fred Perrys, tonic suits, button down shirts and shirts with holes for tie pins, waffle jumpers and cardigans. A trip into town on a Saturday involved going into Huckle's to look at clothes, as well as into the record shops to buy cassettes and pin badges. When you bought clothes at Huckle's, the plastic bag with the Huckle's logo was then used as a school bag. Huckle's was the place to buy your clothes, or rather for my parents to buy my clothes. The cheaper alternative was the weekly market, where I got my pair of maroon Sta-Prest and black waffled V neck. I also had an older cousin who was a mod and I used to get his hand-me-downs. Not bad considering I got a blue Fred Perry V neck jumper, a Tonic jacket and a pair of Dr. Martens boots.

Along with wearing the clothes and having an identity at school, there was a genuine love of the music. Madness made being a Rude Boy accessible to younger children. 'Baggy Trousers' was a song aimed at school kids. I had *One Step Beyond*, both Specials albums and *Dance Craze* on cassette. My favourite band was The Beat. I used to listen to their *Wha'ppen* album and I still do today. The Beat were a political band who wrote songs about racism and growing up in Britain under Mrs Thatcher's government. They played a sophisticated blend of Jamaican, African, reggae, punk and ska music and sung about promoting unity among black and white young people. The band were from the Midlands, the home of the Specials and the Two Tone record label. The Specials wrote songs about inner city violence and looked like 'Gangsters'. The Beat and the Specials made music to make people dance but with a social conscience and message. Whilst I got the music, most of the message went completely over my head. I was too young.

During 1981 and 1982, I went to Vinters Boys High School before taking my 13+ exams and moving onto a Grammar School. At Vinters I was in the same class as Ian. The decision to become a Rude Boy was probably a lot to do with Ian. Ian was a mod and I didn't want to copy him, so my thinking was, *Well, if he's a mod, I'll be a Rude Boy then.* Going into the second year at Vinters I no longer considered myself a Rude Boy. It was a short-lived attraction. I remember going on a school trip to a museum in London and disappearing off with Ian to Carnaby Street. We both purchased and got on the coach home holding 7-inch copies of Benny Spellman's 'Fortune Teller'. From that point on, my love of The Jam, listening to my parents' Kinks records and a new found interest in Northern Soul, meant a new look and new music to get into. However I didn't switch and become a mod then and have never considered myself to be a mod since.

At 41 years old, I am still interested in mod clothes and mod music. There is a dress code that I follow and haven't deviated from for the past 30 years. Fred Perrys, desert boots, Dr. Martens, button-down shirts, Levi's etc. I finally bought a M65 Parka last year when I turned 40. I am also blessed in being a Northern Soul fan, those classic '60s Northern Soul Stompers are surely the best music that's ever been made. Being a Rude Boy for that brief period set me up for a lifelong interest in all things mod. I am still friends with Ian, who asked me to contribute to this book. When we meet up we still talk about the clothes and the music.

Richard Lambert.

★ ★ ★

Sarah Hope, a female Two Tone fan.

It was late May 1979 and our final school year was drawing to a close. We should've all been studying for or GSE and CSE exams, but nahh, we couldn't be bothered. This one night I remember about twenty of us getting on a bus together from the bus station after school (where we used to hang-out of an evening, even after the franchised greasy spoon café in its complex had closed at 9pm), and we were all totally hyper. You see, we were going to a Two-Tone night at the Shrimpers Club in Southend-on-Sea. We had all rushed home from school to change before setting off, and although the boys got their act together quickly, many of us girls were still trying to apply our pitch-black mascara and eye-liner an hour later on our arrival (guess we were just to busy talking and giggling).

I was wearing a black and white chequered mini-dress. I loved this dress. The black and white squares were the size of those on a draft board, and my strawberry blonde hair was held back by a bright white elasticated hair band. My tights were black, and my shoes were white pointed toe patent leather stilettos. A lot of this look was similar in style to the pastel-coloured clothes worn by my Mod friend Debbie, but mine being black and white signified that I was not a Mod but a Rude Girl – a devout follower of Two-Tone music. By the mid-80s, both Debbie and I had become Scooter Girls, however.

Once we had queued with hundreds and hundreds of similarly aged and dressed teenagers (mostly Two-Tone Rudies, but there were many Mods and Skinheads there, too), and parted with our 75p entry fee (that was a lot of money to me in those days), my boyfriend and his mates made straight for the loos where they scored a dozen French Blues, which we then took after a trip to the bar for a pint of bitter for him and a half a sweet cider for me (no one seemed to worry about checking ages too stringently back then).

After this we just skanked our hearts out (skanking was – and is – a style of dance synonymous with Ska and Two Tone music) virtually non-stop, pausing only occasionally to drink another beer and sweet cider respectively. Almost all in attendance were skanking, too. The dance floor was heaving, hot, sticky and sweaty, but above all ELECTRIC.

The DJs spun single after single, and album track after album track from Two-Tone bands like The Specials and Selecta, along with a raft of sounds from many other (then) modern day Two-Tone type performers, too (remember, not all such bands were on the Two-Tone label, for instance Madness were on Stiff and The Beat were on Go Feet).

Debbie and I knew our last bus home was at half past ten, but we were out of our heads on atmosphere, alcohol, adrenalin and amphetamines, so as our witching hour came and went, along with our friends – including our 'soon to be sacked' boyfriends

– Debbie and I hatched a contingency plan, which resulted in us having to wrap scarfs around our heads to simulate crash helmets so we could travel the 30 miles back home riding pillion on the scooters of two male MODS that we knew, who were going our way. This journey home was the catalyst responsible for spawning both my and Debbie's future love affairs with not only the two Knights in Shining Armour who saved us, but also that of the Italian motorscooter (with the latter lasting much MUCH longer)...

Sarah Hope.